EARLE

MICROCOSMOGRAPHY

OR

A PIECE OF THE WORLD DISCOVERED
IN ESSAYS AND CHARACTERS

EDITED BY

HAROLD OSBORNE, M.A.

EDITOR OF BACON: "NEW ATLANTIS"
MARLOWE: "DR FAUSTUS", MORE: "UTOPIA", ETC.

UNIVERSITY TUTORIAL PRESS LTD
Clifton House, Euston Road, London, N.W.1

PREFACE

IN making this edition of the *Microcosmography* my aim has been not merely to produce an edition for the student but to render Earle accessible to the general reading public. It is with this end in view that the spelling and punctuation have been regularised in accordance with modern practice. It is significant of the neglect into which Earle has fallen that hitherto there has been lacking an edition of the *Microcosmography* in modern dress.

The renewal of interest in the literature of the seventeenth century will undoubtedly bring in its train a revival of the literature of Character portrayal, one of the most typical features of seventeenth-century literature. And Earle is the greatest of the writers of Charactery. In my *Introduction* I have endeavoured to set forth the main principles of Charactery and to indicate Earle's position among the other practitioners in this genre. In the *Notes* also I have included parallel quotations from other writers in order to enable the reader to compare and contrast. The intention of the *Notes* throughout is not scholastic but illuminatory. Information is given with the sole purpose of preserving the vitality of the Characters. Therefore I have endeavoured to provide details of contemporary life from which the Characters are drawn—such details as are not ordinarily accessible from the standard textbooks of history. Linguistic notes are included, not to satisfy the grammarian and the philologist, but to enable the reader to savour to the full Earle's delightful use of seventeenth-century " wit."

All editors of Earle are indebted to the edition of Mr. Philip Bliss, a scholarly work now out of print. I have also obtained some assistance from the edition of Mr. A. S. West.

The text has been based upon the edition of 1732, printed by E. Say. This edition is a revival of the sixth edition of 1633, partially corrected and revised by an anonymous editor. This text has been carefully collated with the first edition (1628), and the few variant readings have been noticed.

If this work succeeds in bringing the charm of Earle within the reach of a wider public the labour that it has cost will be well repaid.

H. O.

PRINTED IN GREAT BRITAIN BY UNIVERSITY TUTORIAL PRESS LTD, FOXTON
NEAR CAMBRIDGE

CONTENTS

INTRODUCTION

LIFE AND PERSONALITY.—Of the life of John Earle or Earles, as he himself wrote his name, we know none of those intimate details from which the modern biographer delights to embroider his garish psychological puppets. But to the impression his character made upon those who knew him we have the witness of men whose words must weigh most strongly; and the uniformity of their attestation guarantees to us the impression we ourselves derive of him from the *Microcosmographie*.

The brief facts of the life were first assembled by Dr. Philip Bliss from contemporary sources. His statements have not, I believe, been controverted, and I am not aware that any serious addition has since been made to them.

From his monument, which stands at the north-east corner of Merton College chapel and records his death on the 17th day of November, 1665, in the sixty-fifth year of his age, we gather that John Earle was born in the first year of the seventeenth century. He was sent to Christ Church at the age of about fifteen and there took the degree of Bachelor of Arts, on July 8, 1619. In 1620 he was admitted a probationary fellow at Merton College and in 1624 took the degree of Master of Arts. In 1631 he served as Proctor in the University. About this time he became tutor to Lucius Cary, later Viscount Falkland, and joined the cultured society which gathered at Falkland's country house at Tew.

By his patron, Lord Pembroke, he was brought to the notice of the King, and became chaplain and tutor to Prince Charles at the appointment of Dr. Duppa to the bishopric of Salisbury. In 1642 he took his Doctorate of Divinity and in the following year was invited to be one of the Assembly of Divines appointed by Parliament to remodel the church. This tribute to his recognised fairness and moderation, despite his avowed and unswerving royalist sympathies, is typical of our knowledge of the man. He refused to accept this office, despairing, no doubt, of wielding a useful influence in a body of men with whose objects he had no sympathy.

On the failure of the Royalist cause he was forced to flee the country. He continued high in the favour of the royal family during the exile of Charles II. At the Restoration he was immediately appointed to the Deanery of Westminster. In 1661 he was one of the commissioners appointed to review the Liturgy. In 1662 he was consecrated Bishop of Worcester and in 1663 translated to Salisbury. He died in his apartments at University College, whither he had retired in attendance upon the royal family when the court was transferred to Oxford in order to escape the dangers of the plague.

During his University career Earle seems to have obtained a considerable reputation as a poet, conversationalist and wit. "His younger years," says Wood, "were adorned with oratory, poetry, and witty fancies, and his elder with quaint preaching and subtile disputes." Of these early poems, which he himself wished to suppress, we have few samples. An elegy on Francis Beaumont survives in the folio edition of Beaumont and Fletcher's plays, printed in 1647, but written some "thirty years since" when Earle was sixteen. The following Elegy was written on the death of William Earl of Pembroke, elder brother of Earle's benefactor, in 1630.

Come, Pembroke lives ! Oh ! do not fright our ears
With the destroying truth ! first raise our fears
And say he is not well: that will suffice
To force a river from the public eyes.
Or, if he must be dead, oh ! let the news
Speak in astonish'd whispers: let it use
Some phrase without a voice, and be so told,
As if the labouring sense grieved to unfold
Its doubtful woe. Could not the public zeal
Conquer the Fates, and save yours ? Did the dart
Of death, without a preface, pierce your heart ?
Welcome, sad weeds—but he that mourns for thee,
Must bring an eye that can weep elegy.
A look that could save blacks: whose heavy grace
Chides mirth, and bears a funeral in his face.
Whose sighs are with such feeling sorrows blown,
That all the air he draws returns a groan.
Thou needst no guilded tomb—thy memory,
Is marble to itself—the bravery
Of jem or rich enamel is mis-spent—
Thy noble corpse is its own monument !

We can hardly be mistaken in supposing that the
writer who could compose the verses we have, was
incapable of composing any we should wish to have.
Earle remains for us the author of the " Characters,"
first published in 1628, although they had been
circulating in manuscript for some time previously.
During the earlier part of his exile he was engaged
upon a Latin translation of Hooker's *Ecclesiastical
Polity* and the *Eikon Basilike*.

In Lord Clarendon's *Account of his own life* he
describes Earle as follows:—

" He was a person very notable for his elegance
in the Greek and Latin tongues; and being fellow
of Merton College in Oxford, and having been
proctor of the University, and some very witty and
sharp discourses being published in print without
his consent, though known to be his, he grew sud-
denly into a very general esteem with all men; being
a man of great piety and devotion; a most eloquent

and powerful preacher; and of a conversation so pleasant and delightful, so very innocent, and so very facetious, that no man's company was more desired, and more loved. No man was more negligent in his dress, and habit, and mien; no man more wary and cultivated in his behaviour and discourse; insomuch as he had the greater advantage when he was known, by promising so little before he was known. He was an excellent poet both in Latin, Greek, and English, as appears by many pieces yet abroad; though he suppressed many more himself, especially of English, incomparably good, out of an austerity to those sallies of his youth. He was very dear to the Lord Falkland, with whom he spent as much time as he could make his own; and as that lord would impute the speedy progress he made in the Greek tongue to the information and assistance he had from Mr. Earles, so Mr. Earles would frequently profess that he had got more useful learning by his conversation at Tew (the Lord Falkland's house), than he had at Oxford. In the first settling of the prince his family, he was made one of his chaplains, and attended on him when he was forced to leave the kingdom. He was amongst the few excellent men who never had, and never could have, an enemy, but such a one who was enemy to all learning and virtue, and therefore would never make himself known."

Similar is the testimony of White Kennet, Bishop of Peterborough, who records that Dr. Earle had " this high and rare felicity by his excellent and spotless conversation, to have lived so many years in the court of England, so near his Majesty, and yet not given the least offence to any man alive; though both in and out of pulpit he used all Christian freedom against the vanities of this age, being honoured and admired by all who have either known, heard, or read him."

In his *Life of Mr. Richard Hooker*, Isaac Walton introduces a comparison with Earle: " Dr. Earle, now Lord Bishop of Salisbury, of whom I may justly say, (and let it not offend him, because it is such a thought as ought not to be concealed from posterity, or those that now live and yet know him not,) that, since Mr. Hooker died, none hath lived whom God hath blessed with more innocent wisdom, more sanctified learning, or a more pious peaceable, primitive temper: so that this excellent person seems to be only like himself, and our venerable Richard Hooker."

The *Microcosmography* itself is the best of testimonies to the truth of these impressions.

MICROCOSMOGRAPHIE.—The Characters were first published in 1628 by Edward Blount, to whom they were popularly ascribed until the edition of 1732. From his prefatory note " to the reader " (see page 3) we learn that they had for some while been circulating in manuscript and that Earle was reluctant (" unwillingly willing ") to allow them to be published. The reason for his permission was the danger that some unscrupulous bookseller might publish an unauthorised collection from the copies in circulation (" some very imperfect and surreptitious "). This was a very real danger at the time and Earle had no other safeguard than to publish. We, who benefit by his decision, cannot be too grateful to the perseverance and good taste of Edward Blount—to whom we also owe Marlowe's *Hero and Leander*, Florio's translation of Montaigne's *Essays*, and Shelton's translation of *Don Quixote*. Earle never acknowledged the authorship, and within his lifetime no edition appeared under his name. Yet he was certainly known by his intimates to be the author. It is to the " Characters " that

Clarendon refers when he speaks of " some very witty and sharp discourses."

Three editions of this book were called for in the year of its publication and eight within the lifetime of the author. There were fifty-four Characters in the early editions. Twenty-three were added in the fifth edition (1629). These are: A modest man; A mere empty wit; A drunkard; A prison; A serving man; An insolent man; Acquaintance; A mere complimental man; A poor fiddler; A meddling man; A good old man; A flatterer; A high-spirited man; A mere gull citizen; A lascivious man; A rash man; A profane man; A coward; A sordid rich man; A mere great man; A poor man; An ordinary honest fellow. The Character of A suspicious or jealous man first appeared in the second printing of the sixth edition (1633).

The title *Microcosmographie* means " a description of the little world," and refers to the old idea that man is in himself a miniature embodiment of the universe. Both the word and the idea were popular at the time. In his *History of the World* Sir Walter Raleigh says: " because in the little frame of man's body there is a representation of the Universal; and (by allusion) a kind of participation of all the parts there, therefore was man called *Micro-cosmos*, or the little World." In the *Advancement of Learning*, II. x., § 2, Bacon discusses " the ancient opinion that man was *microcosmus*, an abstract or model of the world." The title is particularly suited to a book of Characters because it may also be interpreted " A *little description* of the world (of man)." The word was used in this sense by Dr. Peter Heylin in his geographical treatise " Μικροκόσμος, *A little description of the Great World.*" Earle combines both meanings, as in the Characters themselves he delights to telescope two meanings of a word into a pun.

CHARACTERY.—For so long as men have been interested in men the description of character and the analysis of characteristics has had a place in literature. But the "character sketch" as an end complete in itself, and an art with strait conventions of its own, belongs, with the solitary exception of Theophrastus, to the seventeenth century. There were of course character sketches before then. Chaucer was a master of charactery. There are Characters written by the Elizabethans—as in Awdeley's and Harman's descriptions of rogues, in Greene's Cony-catching pamphlets, *Quippe for an Upstart Courtier*, etc., and in Nashe. But there was no distinct literary genre with conventions of its own.

The reason for the emergence of this literary genre at the beginning of the seventeenth century has not been explained. Some writers attribute it to the publication by Isaac Casaubon in 1592 of a Latin translation of the Characters of Theophrastus of Lesbos (371–287 B.C.), a pupil of Aristotle, followed in 1593 by an English version of Casaubon's Latin by John Healey. Certain it is that these Characters aroused considerable interest. But it is equally certain that unless the tendency and disposition to Charactery had been already present, they could not have given rise to the stream of books of Charactery which followed. It is, too, easy to exaggerate a supposed "influence" out of relation to the facts. Of the many writers of Charactery, Bishop Hall alone (*Characters of Virtues and Vices*) professedly follows Theophrastus. And he so far misinterprets his model as to regard him primarily as a moral philosopher. Nothing could be further from the unethical observations of that ancient "botanist of minds" than the heavy moralising, the distorted wit, and the scintillating analogies, which obscure what they should elucidate, of Hall. Jonson also knew Theophrastus; but there is no traceable "influence" upon his style of charactery. The other early character-writers—Breton, Stephens, Mynshul, Parrot, Overbury, etc.—are clearly and unmistakeably a natural growth. There could be nothing more preposterous than to trace these individual productions, or the laws which they recognise in their craft, from Casaubon and Healey.

The Elizabethan age was an age of exuberant action and daring creation and discovery; it was followed by an age of meditation and introspection. The literary productions of the latter age are characterised by deep thoughtfulness and serious inspection. It is an age of philosophy and of history and biography. As Mr. Edward Arber says: "In these earlier years of Puritanism especially; and generally throughout the Seventeenth Century, there was a strong passion for analysis of human character. Men delighted in introspection. Essays and Characters took the place of the Romances of the former century." It is noticeable that a similar outcrop of Charactery took place in France during the seventeenth century. The French writing is on the whole more meticulous, more psychological, more detailed; but it lacks the freshness and spontaneity of English Charactery at its best.

The Essay and the Character developed side by side. From the first the Character was a more formal type than the Essay. It had rules and conventions the Essay had not. This is most interestingly illustrated in *Essays and Characters of a Prison and Prisoners*, written in 1617 by Geffray Mynshul in the King's Bench Prison, Southwark. This curious little book contains a number of essays, alternately petulant and pathetic, on prisons, prisoners, jailors, etc., and each essay is followed by a *Character*.

The freedom of the essays contrasts strikingly with the attempted artistry of the Characters.

In the Overbury collection there is a Character of a Character, which is important as a statement of what were accepted as the chief aims and marks of a Character. The three meanings of the word which he gives are: (1) " a deep impression " like a letter of the alphabet; (2) " an impress or short emblem, in little comprehending much "; (3) " a picture (real or personal) quaintly drawn, in various colours, all of them heightened by one shadowing." And these three characteristics must be so combined that, " It is a quaint and soft touch of many strings, all shutting up in one musical close; it is wit's descant on any plain song." With this should be compared another description of a later, and often underrated, writer of Characters. In his *Enigmatical Characters* (1658), Richard Flecknoe has one entitled *Of the Author's Idea, or of a Character.*

" It gives you the hint of discourse, but discourses not; and is that in mass and ingot you may coin and wire-draw to infinite; 'tis more Seneca than Cicero, and speaks rather the language of Oracles than Orators: every line a sentence, and every two a period. It says not all, but all it says is good, and like an Air in Music is either full of closes, or still driving towards a close: 'tis no long-winded exercise of spirit, but a forcible one, and therefore soonest out of breath; 'tis all matter, and to the matter, and has nothing of superfluity, nothing of circumlocution; so little comporting with mediocrity, as it or extols to Heaven or depresses unto Hell; having no mid place for Purgatory left. 'Tis that in every sort of writing delighteth most, and though the Treatise be gold it is the Jewel still, which the Author of Characters, like your Lapidary, produces single, whilst others Goldsmith-like enchase them in their works.

'Tis a Portraiture, not only o' th' Body, but the soul and mind; whence it not only delights but teaches and moves withal, and is a Sermon as well as Picture to everyone.   In fine, 'tis a short voyage, the Writer holds out with equal force, still coming fresh unto his journey's end, whilst in long ones, they commonly tire and falter on their way.   And to the Reader 'tis a garden, not a journey or a feast, where by reason of the subject's variety he is never cloyed but at each Character, as at a new service, falls to with fresh Appetite."

First, a Character is a *picture*, not a *description*. It should be able to be viewed at a glance, as it were. The first essential is therefore *brevity*.   Although the later writers of Charactery tend to lengthen their Characters, the earlier writers seldom exceed the page.   And one feels that this brevity is an essential peculiarity of the genre.   "In long ones they commonly tire and falter on their way."

Secondly, a Character must have *point*.   It is not enough that it should contain " nothing of super-fluity "; each point must be forcibly made.   The main lines of the picture must be vigorously marked. As each point is made it must be sufficient in itself. There may be no elaboration, no " discourse." Hence the style of the Character tends naturally to be epigrammatic—it " speaks rather the language of Oracles than Orators: every line a sentence, and every two a period."

Thirdly, it must have unity and comprehensive-ness.   A collection of points about a type does not constitute a Character.   The colours of the picture must be " heightened by one shadowing."   That is, the points which compose the Character must cohere together in such a way as to produce a single, definite " impression " of the thing characterised.   Not every assemblage of points will do this.   The

Character is, in the strictest sense, a work of art; and the writer of Characters must be an artist. The Character must have unity, form, harmony, completeness. It must be a picture, and not either a photograph or a poster.

Lastly, it was held to be typical of the Character that it should be " quaint " or " conceited." This must not be regarded as *essential*. *London and Country Carbonadoed* (1632), by Donald Lupton, is a collection of scenes of Town and Country life which are among the most interesting of the Characters. There is in them some, though not much, attempt at " wit," and the writer is not successful in the attempt. They claim a high place in the literature of Charactery despite, and not because of, their wit. Yet, in general, Charactery was a humbler expression of the same attitude of mind as produced the metaphysical poetry of the seventeenth century.

In drama and fiction the character is first and foremost *individual*. Its excellence is judged by its individuality, and in this is held to reside its reality. But individuality and universality are abstractions which cease to exist apart from the primary reality which is the character. Granted that the character have sufficient individuality to ensure its reality then its excellence lies in its universality. The great characters of literature are those which, while remaining essentially individual, become universal and belong to all peoples and all time. The subject of the *Character* is always the type, the universal. But it does not differ from drama and fiction as the type differs from the individual. The difference is rather in starting-point and direction. As the character of drama and fiction starts from the individual and creates the universal, so the *Character*, starting from the type, invests it with individuality. The Character was not, and never became, a personification of abstractions, as were the characters in the Moralities. It showed no tendency to fall away towards the scientific or sociological essay. Its aim and its excellence are the individualisation of the type.

The *subjects* of Characterology may be divided into three classes. They are (1) the type of character (a reserved man; a blunt man, etc.); (2) social types (an idle gallant; a shop-keeper, etc.); and (3) places or scenes (a tavern; a bowl alley, etc.). Most Characters fall probably somewhere between these divisions, *e.g.* Characters of An Old Man, Of Spring, of A Downright Scholar, etc. But the classification is as useful as most. It is clear that the subject is always an abstraction, and therefore unreal. There is no such thing as a man who is jealous and nothing more, reserved and nothing more. Jealousy and reserve are abstractions from particular traits manifested by many individual men, by some more and by others less. But always the man is something more than the type, and the type has no separate existence apart from individuals. So there is no such thing as the type of a tavern, a fop, spring, apart from particular taverns and fops and springs. The art of the Character consists in creating individuals while formulating types. A Character is not the picture of the abstract types of Jealousy or Reserve—which do not exist—but the picture of a Jealous *Man* or a Reserved *Man*, who are, none the less, types.

The *method* of charactery cannot be stereotyped. Four methods may be distinguished and these are used in combination or separately. They are: (1) formulation of typical characteristics; (2) formulation of typical behaviour; (3) analogy and simile; (4) anecdote. But any classification such as this must give a too wooden idea of the variety and vitality of the actual writings. And no rules can be laid down. So long as the writer creates a *picture* of a type, that is a Character which is individual, he has succeeded in his art.

EARLE AS CHARACTEROLOGIST.—Charactery proved a literary genre particularly liable to abuse. In its most genuine form the Character is the outcome of the pure interest in artistic portrayal. But the form proved a convenient vehicle for other interests. So early as Hall the pure interest of Charactery was combined with the subsidiary interest of moralisation, and his Characters have something of the odour of sermons. Didacticism continued throughout the century a potent distorting influence. Again, the Character was soon found to be a useful vehicle for satire and invective. It has been used for royalist flattery by Wortley, and in an anonymous little volume of characters of animals, whose title is *A Strange Metamorphosis of Man transformed into a Wildernesse* (1634), it becomes pure phantasy. The majority of the later writers, including Butler in many of his pieces, err in preferring satire to objective portrayal. Not that a satirical Character is necessarily a bad Character; but the satirical Character in general, to the pure Character as found in Earle at his best, is as the caricature to the portrait.

The most serious distortion, however, which was present from the first, is in the realm of style. " Wit " was the literary characteristic of the age, and the Character was closely associated with wit. So long as wit remains a method only, and is subordinated to the main purpose of the Character, no association could be more happy. But inevitably the importance of wit was exaggerated and the Character often became a mere exercise in wit. The justification of many Characters is simply and

solely their wit. So long as the wit is at a high
level they may still be amusing, though perhaps not
of high literary value. But when the wit itself is
ponderous or extravagant, the Character has touched
the depths of banality.

The genius of Earle, in whom Charactery found
its finest artist, will be most nicely appreciated by
contrast with the perversions just mentioned. In
him we see the pure artistic interest in portrayal.
His subjects are less whimsically chosen than those
of the Overbury collection and of almost any later
volume. If the Characters are arranged under
classes, each one will be found to portray either a
distinct and common type of personality, or a
distinct social type, or, in the case of the Tavern,
Bowl Alley, Prison, and Paul's Walk, places which
have, as it were, an obvious character inviting
portrayal. Indeed the most noticeable thing about
his titles is that each one subject is recognised to be
typical and to have distinctness and character; there
is demanded no effort of wit or whimsicality to force
a character upon them. And when the circum-
stances of composition and publication are taken
into account, the completeness of the volume is
more admired than its necessary fragmentariness.
The preponderance of university and scholastic
types is a natural result of the environment and
occupation of the author.

Each Character has artistic balance and finish.
Each one is a miniature and not an incident snipped
away from a larger canvass. This quality is perhaps
more strikingly evident in the slighter Characters,
such as those of the Baker, the Tobacco-Seller, etc.
The general insight of the writer is remarkable for
balance and poise. Sound judgement and psychological penetration make the portraits of types of
character geniune psychological documents. And

Earle had that rare gift of the true artist, the ability to isolate and display the salient characteristics which in proper combination constitute the essence of the type. He can make use of sarcasm, but sarcasm is never an end in itself. He can be merciless in ridicule (as in the Character of the Young Raw Preacher) but only when the ridiculousness lies in the type itself. His Character of A Young Man is obviously one-sided. But Youth is too various and many-sided to become the subject of a single Character, and Earle's choice of one aspect implies no denial of the other aspects. Over against this we have his Character of the Old Man; the beauty of this Character, its humanity and fineness, contrasted with the easy ridicule of the other writers on Old Age, would alone prove his superiority. Earle is among all the writers of Charactery the sage without cynicism.

Earle and not Hall is the true descendant of Theophrastus. Hall looks at the world through the moralist's spectacles and with so distorted a vision that he sees even Theophrastus himself as a moralist. Earle has the genuine artist's interest and ability to see things as they are. No irrelevant bias or uncongenial preoccupation obscures his vision or impedes the artistry of his portrayal. In his objectivity he recaptures the spirit of his master. It is a sign of his originality that, although he must with his classical education and his interest in Charactery have studied Theophrastus, he nowhere directly imitates him. There are no passages of which one could say that they were derived from Theophrastus rather than from Earle's own observations. The chief methodological difference between them is that Theophrastus portrays rather by describing what his characters do in particular cases, while Earle prefers to describe what they do in general. The difference is not, however, more than a tendency and should not be pressed unduly.

Earle, too, had more of the analytic insight of Theophrastus than any of his fellows. He is the most psychological of all English literary writers of Charactery. Consider the last three sentences of the *Plausible Man*, the last sentence of the *Blunt Man*, the subtle analysis of the stages of ingratiation of the *Flatterer*, the fine distinctions between the *Flatterer*, the *Plausible Man*, the *Complimenter*, and the *Partial Man*, and so on. In contrast with Butler, who accepts conventional psychological analyses, the analyses of Earle have the freshness of originality and direct observation. And finally, as a psychologist, Earle is *comprehensive* in his characterisation. He does not select two or three points and enlarge upon them, but selects the salient features of a type and moulds them into a creative unity. Rarely do we find two sentences devoted to the same characteristic. Butler, again in contrast, often uses six or seven sentences to impress the same point in a variety of ways, and often gives but three or four points in a whole Character. It is in this sureness and freedom from repetition that one sees the rapidity and artistry of Earle's Characters.

STYLE.—The terseness of the Character itself is reflected in the style. There is no periodic structure anywhere in Charactery. The sentence is composed of a set of short and pointed clauses juxtaposed and not interwoven. Often the Character itself is composed of such clauses, separated by colons, semi-colons, full-stops, or commas according to the fancy of the printer of each edition. In the formation of the clause ellipsis is cultivated to the limit of possibility. Earle's stylistic brevity is masterly and unforced. He is almost never strained or obscure;

he is never diffuse. To the modern reader he appears difficult only in the few instances where modern habits in the use of ellipsis have differed from those of his day. Yet even in those cases the perspicacity of his thought and the logical lucidity of his language prevent real obscurity.

The brevity of style falls naturally into epigram, and Earle has epigrams in most of his Characters. Their excellence will best be appreciated if they are remembered in isolation from their context. An epigram strikes the mind most vigorously when it occurs in a passage of smooth and relatively undifferentiated regularity; it appeals by *contrast* with the level flow of its context; and in a style which perpetually verges upon the epigrammatic that contrast is absent. Earle did not use his epigrams as the modern writer uses his; he never creates that sense of shock which makes us pause and savour the modern epigram. His epigrams are organic to his style.

In wit also Earle is scintillating, precise, and felicitous. But his wit, like his epigram, arises naturally from his subject and merges harmoniously in his style. With him style is never the main interest; it is used in the interests of portraiture. One is never caused to feel that the portrait was written in order to provide excuse for stylistic brilliance. Of the Hypocrite Hall says: " He is the stranger's saint, the neighbour's disease, the blot of goodness, a rotten stick on a dark night, a poppy in a cornfield, an ill-tempered candle with a great snuff that in going out smells ill; an angel abroad, a devil at home, and worse when an angel than a devil." Overbury opens his Character of A Puritan with " Is a diseased piece of Apocrypha." These are mere verbal fireworks. They do not serve the interests of characterisation, but exist because of their intrinsic brilliance. Earle is not less brilliant, but is more artistic.

Finally, Earle almost alone among the writers of Charactery has humour. Humour is a quality which does not easily coexist with wit. Earle's humour is genuine, subtle, enjoyable. Such Characters as those of the *Baker* have a charm which is pure humour. Everywhere humour is combined with quiet irony. Where Overbury is cruel and almost vindictive in his sarcasm, Earle is suave in his irony. The Characters of the *She Precise Hypocrite* and the *Pretender to Learning* are among the masterpieces of ironic humour in our language. The only other Character which I know that can be compared with Earle in this quality is Flecknoe's *Old Gentlewoman*.

A word should perhaps be said about Earle's use of the pun. To-day the pun is repudiated as worthy only of schoolboy facetiousness. So long as the pun is regarded as attempted humour, it will stand as an obstacle to appreciation. It is an accepted and permanent literary device of Charactery; but never, I believe, is it used with humorous intent. It belongs to the sphere of wit. The modern repudiation of the pun is a natural consequence of the decay of wit. Earle's use of the pun must therefore be judged as we judge his use of wit. And by this standard it will be found always to add piquancy and point to characterisation; seldom to be introduced as an end in itself; and never to obscure or impede the main purpose of the Character.

THE CHARACTER TO-DAY.—The Character was perpetuated in the following century in the periodical essay. From the pens of Steele, Addison, Goldsmith we have Characters drawn with delicacy and charm. Even the great Dr. Johnson was moved with laborious sprightliness to create Dick Minim.

Although most of these Characters were written in furtherance of the high moral purpose which gave birth to the *Tatler* and *Spectator*, they are not obviously or offensively didactic. They differ from the Charactery of the previous century in adapting the style of the essay to the purpose of portrayal. The conventions of Charactery go by the board. And the Character is always *named*, even though it be a pure portrayal of type.

The essay-Character in turn gave place to, as it had made possible, the Character of the novel. The Characters of Steele, Addison, and their friends were still often types although usually thinly disguised as particular individuals. We also get definitely individual characters, such as Sir Roger, Will Wimble, Mrs. Slipslop, etc. In the novel the Character is again frankly individual. Modern Charactery, with isolated exceptions, is the portrayal of individuals. They may be typical, as Pecksniff is typical of the hypocrite, but their individuality is primary. This is true even of recent Character sketches which are not novels—of the Characters in *Sketches by Boz*, *Theophrastus Such*, and the *Book of Snobs*. They are *novel* Characters and not Characters such as Earle drew.

This does not detract from Earle's importance to-day. The interest of an artist consummate in his own craft is perpetual, and an art which has produced such successful achievements as his has permanent importance. It may be that as, in the revolt from the Romantic Revival, the metaphysical poets have come into their own, so a new interest in " wit " may make possible a fresh realisation of the possibilities of Charactery. Earle's Characters, drawn upon the models of his own age, are for all time. I cannot do better than conclude this brief introduction with some words from the anonymous editor who

tried in 1732, without success, to reinstate Earle in
the position he deserves to hold in the affections of
his countrymen. " The Change of Fashions un-
avoidably casts a Shade upon a few places, yet even
those contain an exact Picture of the Age wherein
they were written, as the rest does of Mankind in
general: for Reflections founded upon Nature will
be just in the main, as long as Men are Men, tho'
the particular Instances of Vice and Folly be
diversified. *Paul's Walk* is now no more, but then
good Company adjourn to Coffee-Houses, and at the
reasonable Fine of two or three pence throw away
as much of their precious Time as they find troublesome. Perhaps these Valuable Essays may be as
acceptable to the Publick now, as they were at first;
both for the Entertainment of those who are already
experienced in the Ways of Mankind, and for the
Information of others who would know the World
in the best way, that is without trying it."

Micro-cofmographie,

OR,

A PEECE OF
THE WORLD
DISCOVERED ;

IN ESSAYES AND
Characters.

LONDON,
Printed by *William Stansby* for
Edward Blount, 1628.

TO
THE READER
GENTEEL OR GENTLE

I HAVE (for once) adventured to play the mid-wife's part, helping to bring forth these infants into the world, which the father would have smothered: who having left them lapt up in loose sheets, as soon as his fancy was delivered of them; written especially for his private recreation, to pass away the time in the country, and by the forcible request of friends drawn from him; yet passing severally from hand to hand in written copies, grew at length to be a pretty number in a little volume: and among so many sundry dispersed transcripts, some very imperfect and surreptitious had like to have passed the press, if the author had not used speedy means of prevention: when, perceiving the hazard he ran to be wronged, was unwillingly willing to let them pass as now they appear to the world. If any faults have escaped the press, (as few books can be printed without) impose them not on the author I intreat thee; but rather impute them to mine and the printer's oversight, who seriously promise on the re-impression hereof, by greater care and diligence, for this our former default to make thee ample satisfaction. In the meanwhile, I remain

Thine.

ED. BLOUNT

A TABLE OF
CONTENTS

MICROCOSMOGRAPHY

OR, A PIECE OF THE WORLD CHARACTERIZED

1. A CHILD

Is a Man in a small letter, yet the best copy of Adam before he tasted of Eve or the apple; and he is happy whose small practice in the world can only write his character. He is nature's fresh picture newly drawn in oil, which time and much handling dims and defaces. His Soul is yet a white paper unscribbled with observations of the world, wherewith at length it becomes a blurred note-book. He is purely happy, because he knows no evil, nor hath made means by sin to be acquainted with misery. He arrives not at the mischief of being wise, nor endures evils to come by foreseeing them. He kisses and loves all, and when the smart of the rod is past, smiles on his beater. Nature and his parents alike dandle him, and tice him on with a bait of sugar to a draught of wormwood. He plays yet, like a young prentice the first day, and is not come to his task of melancholy. All the language he speaks yet is tears, and they serve him well enough to express his necessity. His hardest labour is his tongue, as if he were loath to use so deceitful an organ; and he is best company with it when he can but prattle. We laugh at his foolish sports, but his game is our earnest; and his drums, rattles and hobby-horses but the emblems and mocking of men's business. His father hath writ him as his own little story, wherein he reads those days of his life that he cannot remember, and sighs to see what innocence he has out-lived. The older he grows, he is a stair lower from God; and like his first father much worse in his breeches. He is the Christian's example, and the old man's relapse; the one imitates his pureness, and the other falls into his simplicity. Could he put off his body with his little coat he had got eternity without a burthen and exchanged but one heaven for another.

2. A YOUNG RAW PREACHER

Is a Bird not yet fledged, that hath hopped out of his nest to be chirping on a hedge, and will be straggling abroad at what peril soever. His backwardness in the University hath set him thus forward; for had he not truanted there, he had not been so hasty a Divine. His small standing and time hath made him a proficient only in boldness, out of which and his table-book he is furnished for a preacher. His collections of study are the notes of sermons, which taken up at St. Mary's he utters in the country. And if he write brachigraphy, his stock is so much the better. His writing is more than his reading; for he reads only what he gets without book. Thus accomplished he comes down to his friends, and his first salutation is grace and peace out of the pulpit. His prayer is conceited, and no man remembers his College more at large. The pace of his sermon is a full career, and he runs wildly over hill and dale till the clock stop him. The labour of it is chiefly in his lungs; and the only thing he has made of it himself is the faces. He takes on against the Pope without mercy, and has a jest still in lavender for Bellarmine; yet he preaches heresy, if it comes in his way, though with a mind I must needs say very orthodox. His action is all passion, and his speech interjections. He has an excellent faculty in bemoaning the people, and spits with a very good grace. His style is compounded of some twenty several men's, only his body imitates some one extraordinary. He will not draw his handkercher out of his place, nor blow his nose without discretion. His commendation is, that he never looks upon book; and indeed, he was never used to it. He preaches but once a year, though twice on Sunday; for the stuff is still the same, only the dressing a little altered. He has more tricks with a sermon than a tailor with an old cloak, to turn it, and piece it, and at last quite disguise it with a new preface. If he have waded farther in his profession, and would shew reading of his own, his authors are postils, and his School-divinity a catechism. His fashion and demure habit gets him in with some Town-precisian and makes him a guest on Friday nights. You shall know him by his narrow velvet cape and serge facing, and his ruff, next his hair the shortest thing about him. The companion of his walk is some zealous tradesman, whom he astonisheth with strange points, which they both understand alike. His friends and much painfulness may prefer him to thirty pounds a year, and this means, to a chambermaid; with whom we leave him now in the bonds of wedlock. Next Sunday you shall have him again.

3. A GRAVE DIVINE

Is one that knows the burthen of his calling, and
hath studied to make his shoulders sufficient; for
which he hath not been hasty to launch forth of his
port the University, but expected the ballast of
learning and the wind of opportunity. Divinity is
not the beginning but the end of his studies, to which
he takes the ordinary stair, and makes the Arts his
way. He counts it not profaneness to be polished
with humane reading, or to smooth his way by
Aristotle to School-divinity. He has sounded both
religions and anchored in the best, and is a Protestant
out of judgement not faction, not because his country
but his reason is on this side. The ministry is his
choice not refuge, and yet the Pulpit not his itch but
fear. His discourse there is substance, not all
rhetoric, and he utters more things than words.
His speech is not helped with enforced action, but
the matter acts itself. He shoots all his meditations
at one butt; and beats upon his text, not the cushion,
making his hearers, not the pulpit groan. In citing
of Popish errors he cuts them with arguments, not
cudgels them with barren invectives; and labours more
to shew the truth of his cause than the spleen. His
sermon is limited by the method, not the hour-glass;
and his devotion goes along with him out of the
pulpit. He comes not up thrice a week because he
would not be idle, nor talks three hours together
because he would not talk nothing: but his tongue
preaches at fit times and his conversation is the every
day's exercise. In matters of ceremony he is not
ceremonious, but thinks he owes that reverence to
the Church to bow his judgement to it, and make
more conscience of schism than a surplice. He
esteems the Church's Hierarchy as the Church's

glory, and however we jar with Rome would not have our confusion distinguish us. In simoniacal purchases he thinks his soul goes in the bargain, and is loath to come by promotion so dear. Yet his worth at the length advances him, and the price of his own merit buys him a living. He is no base grater of his tythes, and will not wrangle for the odd egg. The lawyer is the only man he hinders, by whom he is spited for taking up quarrels. He is a main pillar of our Church, though not yet Dean or Canon, and his life our Religion's best Apology. His death is his last sermon, where in the pulpit of his bed he instructs men to die by his example.

4. A MODEST MAN

Is a far finer man than he knows of, one that shews better to all men than himself, and so much the better to all men as less to himself; for no quality sets a man off like this, and commends him more against his will: and he can put up any injury sooner than this (as he calls it), your irony. You shall hear him confute his commenders, and giving reasons how much they are mistaken, and is angry almost if they do not believe him. Nothing threatens him so much as great expectation, which he thinks more prejudicial than your under-opinion, because it is easier to make that false than this true. He is one that sneaks from a good action as one that had pilfered, and dare not justify it, and is more blushingly deprehended in this than others in sin: That counts all public declarings of himself but so many penances before the people; and the more you applaud him the more you abash him, and he recovers not his face a month after. One that is easy to like anything of another man's, and thinks all he knows not of him better than that he knows. He excuses that to you which another would impute; and if you pardon him is satisfied. One that stands in no opinion because it is his own, but suspects it rather because it is his own, and is confuted and thanks you. He sees nothing more willingly than his errors; and it is his error sometimes to be too soon persuaded. He is content to be auditor where he only can speak, and content to go away and think himself instructed. No man is so weak that he is ashamed to learn of, and is less ashamed to confess it; and he finds many times even in the dust what others overlook and lose. Every man's presence is a kind of bridle to him, to stop the roving of his tongue and passions: and even impudent men look for this reverence from him, and distaste that in him which they suffer in themselves, as one in whom vice is ill-favoured, and shews more scurvily than another. A bawdy jest shall shame him more than a bastard another man, and he that got it shall censure him among the rest. And he is a coward to nothing more than an ill tongue, and whosoever dare lie on him hath power over him; and if you take him by his look, he is guilty. The main ambition of his life is not to be discredited; and for other things, his desires are more limited than his fortunes, which he thinks preferment though never so mean, and that he is to do something to deserve this. He is too tender to venture on great places, and would not hurt a dignity to help himself: If he do, it was the violence of his friends constrained him; and how hardly soever he obtain it, he was harder persuaded to seek it.

5. A MERE DULL PHYSICIAN

His practice is some business at bedsides, and his speculation an urinal. He is distinguished from an Empiric by a round velvet cap and Doctor's gown, yet no man takes degrees more superfluously, for he is Doctor howsoever. He is sworn to Galen and Hypocrates, as University men to their Statutes, though they never saw them: and his discourse is all Aphorisms, though his reading be only Alexis of Piedmont or the *Regiment of Health.* The best cure he has done is upon his own purse, which from a lean sickliness he hath made lusty and in flesh. His learning consists much in reckoning up the hard names of diseases, and the superscriptions of gally-pots in his Apothecary's shop, which are ranked in his shelves, and the Doctor's memory. He is indeed only languaged in diseases, and speaks Greek many times when he knows not. If he have been but a bystander at some desperate recovery, he is slandered with it though he be guiltless; and this breeds his reputation, and that his practice; for his skill is merely opinion. Of all odours he likes best the smell of urine and holds Vespatian's rule, that no gain is unsavoury. If you send this once to him you must resolve to be sick howsoever, for he will never leave examining your water till he have shaked it into a disease. Then follows a writ to his drugger in a strange tongue, which he understands though he cannot construe. If he see you himself, his presence is the worst visitation: for if he cannot heal your sickness, he will be sure to help it. He translates his Apothecary's shop into your chamber, and the very windows and benches must take physic. He tells you your malady in Greek, though it be but a cold, or headache; which by good endeavour and diligence he may bring to some moment indeed; his most unfaithful act is that he leaves a man gasping, and his pretence is, death and he have a quarrel and must not meet; but his fear is lest the carcass should bleed. Anatomies and other spectacles of mortality have hardened him, and he is no more struck with a funeral than a gravemaker. Noblemen use him for a director of their stomach, and ladies for wantonness, especially if he be a proper man. If he be single, he is in league with his she-apothecary; and because it is the Physician the husband is Patient. If he have leisure to be idle (that is to study) he has a smatch at Alchemy, and is sick of the Philosopher's stone, a disease uncurable but by an abundant phlebotomy of the purse. His two main opposites are a mountebank and a good woman, and he never shews his learning so much as in an invective against them and their boxes. In conclusion, he is a sucking consumption himself, and a very brother to the worms, for they are both engendered out of man's corruption.

6. A MERE EMPTY WIT

Is like one that spends on the stock without any revenues coming in, and will shortly be no wit at all; for learning is the fuel to this fire of wit, which if it wants this feeding, eats out itself. A good conceit or two bates of such a man and makes a sensible weakening in him; and his brain recovers it not a year after. The rest of him are bubbles and flashes, darted out on the sudden, which if you take them while they are warm, may be laughed at; if they cool, are nothing. He speaks best on the present apprehension, for meditation stupifies him and the more he is in travail the less he brings forth. His things come off then, as in a nauseating stomach, where there is nothing to cast up—strains and convulsions, and some astonishing bombast, which men only till they understand are scared with. A verse or some such work he may sometimes get up to, but seldom above the stature of an Epigram, and that with some relief out of Martial, which is the ordinary companion of his pocket, and he reads him as he were inspired. Such men are commonly the trifling things of the world, good to make merry the company, and whom only men have to do withal when they have nothing to do, and none are less their friends than who are most their company. Here they vent themselves o'er a cup somewhat more lastingly; all their words go for jests, and all their jests for nothing. They are nimble in the fancy of some ridiculous thing, and reasonable good in the expression. Nothing stops a jest when it's coming, neither friends nor danger, but it must out howsoever, though their blood come out after, and then they emphatically rail and are emphatically beaten, and commonly are men reasonable familiar to this.

E. M.   2

Briefly they are such whose life is but to laugh and be laughed at; and only wits in jest, and fools in earnest.

7. A MERE ALDERMAN

He is venerable in his gown; more in his beard, wherewith he sets not forth so much his own, as the face of a City. You must look on him as one of the Town Gates, and consider him not as a Body but a Corporation. His eminency above others hath made him a man of worship, for he had never been preferred but that he was worth thousands. He oversees the Commonwealth as his shop, and it is an argument of his policy that he has thriven by his craft. He is a rigorous magistrate in his ward: yet his scale of justice is suspected, lest it be like the balances in his warehouse. A ponderous man is he, and substantial: for his weight is commonly extraordinary, and in his preferment nothing rises so much as his belly. His head is of no great depth, yet well furnished; and when it is in conjunction with his brethren, may bring forth a City Apophthegm, or some such sage matter. He is one that will not hastily run into error, for he treads with great deliberation, and his judgement consists much in his pace. His discourse is commonly the Annals of his Mayoralty, and what good government there was in the days of his gold chain: though his door-posts were the only things that suffered reformation. He seems most sincerely religious, especially on solemn days; for he comes often to Church to make a show, and is a part of the quire hangings. He is the highest stair of his profession, and an example to his trade what in time they may come to. He makes very much of his authority, but more of his satin doublet; which though of good years bears its age very well, and looks fresh every Sunday. But his scarlet gown is a monument and lasts from generation to generation.

8. A DISCONTENTED MAN

Is one that is fallen out with the world and will be revenged on himself. Fortune has denied him in something, and he now takes pet and will be miserable in spite. The root of his disease is a self-humouring pride and an accustomed tenderness not to be crossed in his fancy; and the occasions commonly one of these three, a hard father, a peevish wench, or his ambition thwarted. He considered not the nature of the world till he felt it, and all blows fall on him heavier because they light not first on his expectation. He has now forgone all but his pride, and is yet vainglorious in the ostentation of his melancholy. His composure of himself is a studied carelessness, with his arms across and a neglected hanging of his head and cloak, and he is as great an enemy to an hatband as fortune. He quarrels at the time, and upstarts, and sighs at the neglect of men of parts, that is, such as himself. His life is a perpetual satire, and he is still girding the age's vanity; when this very anger shews he too much esteems it. He is much displeased to see men merry and wonders what they can find to laugh at. He never draws his own lips higher than a smile and frowns wrinkle him before forty. He at the last falls into that deadly melancholy to be a bitter hater of men, and is the most apt companion for any mischief. He is the spark that kindles the Commonwealth, and the bellows himself to blow it: and if he turn any thing, it is commonly one of these, either Friar, Traitor, or Madman.

9. AN ANTIQUARY

He is a man strangely thrifty of time past, and an enemy indeed to his maw, whence he fetches out many things when they are now all rotten and stinking. He is one that hath that unnatural disease to be enamoured of old age and wrinkles, and loves all things (as Dutchmen do cheese) the better for being mouldy and worm-eaten. He is of our Religion because we say it is most ancient; and yet a broken statue would almost make him an idolater. A great admirer he is of the rust of old monuments, and reads only those characters where time hath eaten out the letters. He will go you forty miles to see a Saint's Well or ruined Abbey; and if there be but a cross or stone foot-stool in the way, he'll be considering it so long, till he forget his journey. His estate consists much in shekels and Roman coins, and he hath more pictures of Caesar than James or Elizabeth. Beggars cozen him with musty things which they have raked from dunghills, and he preserves their rags for precious relics. He loves no library but where there are more spiders' volumes than authors', and looks with great admiration on the antique work of cobwebs. Printed books he contemns, as a novelty of this latter age; but a Manuscript he pores on everlastingly, especially if the cover be all moth-eaten, and the dust make a parenthesis between every syllable. He would give all the books in his study (which are rarities all) for one of the old Roman binding or six lines of Tully in his own hand. His chamber is hung commonly with strange beasts' skins, and is a kind of charnelhouse of bones extraordinary; and his discourse upon them, if you will hear him, shall last longer. His very attire is that which is the eldest out of fashion, and you may pick a criticism out of his breeches. He never looks upon himself till he is gray-haired, and then he is pleased with his own antiquity. His grave does not fright him for he has been used to sepulchres, and he likes death the better because it gathers him to his fathers.

10. A DRUNKARD

Is one that will be a man to-morrow morning, but is now what you will make him, for he is in the power of the next man, and if a friend the better.

One that hath let go himself from the hold and stay of reason, and lies open to the mercy of all temptations. No lust but finds him disarmed and fenceless, and with the least assault enters. If any mischief escape him it was not his fault, for he was laid as fair for it as he could. Every man sees him, as Cham saw his father, the first of this sin, an uncovered man, and though his garment be on, uncovered; the secretest parts of his soul lying in the nakedest manner visible: all his passions come out now, all his vanities, and those shamefuller humours which discretion clothes. His body becomes at last like a miry way, where the spirits are be-clogged and cannot pass: all his members are out of office, and his heels do but trip up one another. He is a blind man with eyes, and a cripple with legs on. All the use he has of this vessel himself, is to hold thus much; for his drinking is but a scooping in of so many quarts, which are filled out into his body, and that filled out again into the room, which is commonly as drunk as he. Tobacco serves to air him after a washing, and is his only breath, and breathing while. He is the greatest enemy to himself and the next to his friend, and then most in the act of his kindness, for his kindness is but trying a mastery, who shall sink down first: and men come from him as from a battle, wounded and bound up. Nothing takes a man off more from his credit and business, and makes him more recklessly careless what becomes of all. Indeed he dares not enter on a serious thought, or if he do, it is such melancholy that it sends him to be drunk again.

11. A YOUNGER BROTHER

His elder brother was the Esau that came out first and left him like Jacob at his heels. His father has done with him as Pharaoh to the children of Israel, that would have them make brick and give them no straw, so he tasks him to be a Gentleman and leaves him nothing to maintain it. The pride of his house has undone him, which the elder's Knighthood must sustain, and his beggary that Knighthood. His birth and bringing up will not suffer him to descend to the means to get wealth: but he stands at the mercy of the world, and, which is worse, of his brother. He is something better than the servingmen; yet they more saucy with him than he bold with the master, who beholds him with a countenance of stern awe, and checks him oftener than his liveries. His brother's old suits and he are much alike in request, and cast off now and then one to the other. Nature hath furnished him with a little more wit upon compassion; for it is like to be his best revenue. If his annuity stretch so far, he is sent to the University, and with great heart-burning takes upon him the Ministry, as a profession he is condemned to by his ill fortune. Others take a more crooked path yet, the King's highway, where at length their vizard is plucked off, and they strike fair for Tyburn: but their brother's pride, not love, gets them a pardon. His last refuge is the Low Countries, where rags and lice are no scandal, where he lives a poor Gentleman of a company, and dies without a shirt. The only thing that may better his fortunes is an art he has to make a Gentlewoman, wherewith he baits now and then some rich widow that is hungry after his blood. He is commonly discontented, and desperate, and the form of his exclamation is, "that Churl my Brother." He loves

not his Country for this unnatural custom, and
would have long since revolted to the Spaniard but
for Kent only, which he holds in admiration.

12. A MERE FORMAL MAN

Is somewhat more than the shape of a man; for
he has his length, breadth, and colour. When you
have seen his outside you have looked through him
and need employ your discovery no farther. His
reason is merely example and his action is not
guided by his understanding, but he sees other men
do thus, and he follows them. He is a Negative,
for we cannot call him a wise man, but not a fool;
nor an honest man, but not a knave; nor a Protestant,
but not a Papist. The chief burden of his brain is
the carriage of his body and the setting of his face
in a good frame; which he performs the better,
because he is not disjointed with other meditations.
His religion is a good quiet subject, and he prays as
he swears, in the phrase of the land. He is a fair
guest and a fair inviter, and can excuse his good
cheer in the accustomed apology. He has some
faculty in mangling of a rabbit and the distribution
of his morsel to a neighbour's trencher. He apprehends a jest by seeing men smile, and laughs orderly
himself when it comes to his turn. His businesses
with his friends are to visit them, and whilst the
business is no more, he can perform this well enough.
His discourse is the news that he hath gathered in
his walk, and for other matters his discretion is

that he will only what he can, that is, say nothing.
His life is like one that runs to the Church-walk to
take a turn or two, and so passes. He hath stayed
in the world to fill a number; and when he is gone
there wants one, and there's an end.

13. A CHURCH-PAPIST

Is one that parts his Religion betwixt his conscience
and his purse, and comes to Church not to serve God
but the King. The face of the Law makes him
wear the mask of the Gospel, which he uses not as
a means to save his soul but charges. He loves
Popery well, but is loath to lose by it; and though he
be something scared with the Bulls of Rome, yet
they are far off, and he is struck with more terror at
the apparitor. Once a month he presents himself
at the Church, to keep off the Church-warden, and
brings in his body to save his bail. He kneels with
the congregation, but prays by himself, and asks God
forgiveness for coming thither. If he be forced to
stay out a Sermon, he pulls his hat over his eyes
and frowns out the hour; and when he comes home
thinks to make amends for his fault by abusing the
preacher. His main policy is to shift off the Communion, for which he is never unfurnished of a
quarrel, and will be sure to be out of Charity at
Easter; and indeed he lies not, for he has a quarrel
to the Sacrament. He would make a bad martyr,
and a good traveller, for his conscience is so large
he could never wander out of it, and in Constantinople

would be circumcised with a reservation. His wife is more zealous, and therefore more costly, and he bates her in tires what she stands him in religion. But we leave him hatching plots against the state, and expecting Spinola.

14. A PRISON

Is the grave of the living, where they are shut up from the world and their friends; and the worms that gnaw upon them their own thoughts and the jailor. A house of meagre looks and ill smells, for lice, drink, tobacco are the compound. Pluto's court was expressed from this fancy; and the persons are much about the same parity that is there. You may ask, as Menippus in Lucian, which is Nireus, which Thersites, which the Beggar, which the Knight; for they are all suited in the same form of a kind of nasty poverty. Only to be out at elbows is in fashion here, and a great indecorum not to be threadbare. Every man shows here like so many wrecks upon the sea, here the ribs of a thousand pound, here the relic of so many manors, a doublet without buttons. And 'tis a spectacle of more pity than executions are. The company one with the other is but a vying of complaints and the causes they have to rail on fortune and fool themselves, and there is a great deal of good fellowship in this. They are commonly, next their creditors, most bitter against the lawyers, as men that have had a great stroke in assisting them hither. Mirth here is stupidity or hard-heartedness, yet they feign it sometimes to slip melancholy and keep off themselves from themselves, and the torment of thinking what they have been. Men huddle up their life here as a thing of no use, and wear it out like an old suit, the faster the better; and he that deceives the time best, best spends it. It is the place where new comers are most welcomed, and next them ill news, as that which extends their fellowship in misery, and leaves fewer to insult. And they breathe their discontents more securely here, and have their tongues at more liberty than abroad. Men see here much sin and much calamity; and where the last does not mortify, the other hardens; and those that are worse here are desperately worse, as those from whom the horror of sin is taken off, and the punishment familiar: and commonly a hard thought passes on all that come from this school; which though it teach much wisdom, it is too late, and with danger: and it is better be a fool than come here to learn it.

15. A SELF-CONCEITED MAN

Is one that knows himself so well that he does not know himself. Two excellent *well-dones* have undone him; and he is guilty, that first commended him to madness. He is now become his own book, which he pores on continually, yet like a truant-reader skips over the harsh places and surveys only that which is pleasant. In the speculation of his own good parts his eyes, like a drunkard's, see all double, and his fancy, like an old man's spectacles, makes a great letter in a small print. He imagines every place where he comes his theatre, and not a look stirring, but his spectator; and conceives men's thoughts to be very idle, that is, only busy about him. His walk is still in the fashion of a march, and, like his opinion, unaccompanied, with his eyes most fixed upon his own person, or on others with reflection to himself. If he have done anything that has passed with applause, he is always re-acting it alone, and conceits the ecstasy his hearers were in at every period. His discourse is all positions and definitive decrees, with " thus it must be " and " thus it is," and he will not humble his authority to prove it. His tenet is always singular and aloof from the vulgar as he can, from which you must not hope to wrest him. He has an excellent humour for an heretic, and in these days made the first Arminian. He prefer Ramus before Aristotle, and Paracelsus before Galen, and whosoever with most paradox is commended, [and Lipsius his hopping stile, before either Tully or Quintilian]. He much pities the world, that has no more insight in his parts, when he is too well discovered even to this very thought. A flatterer is a dunce to him, for he can tell him nothing but what he knows before; and yet he loves him too, because he is like himself. Men are merciful to him and let him alone, for if he be once driven from his humour he is like two inward friends fallen out; his own bitter enemy and discontent presently makes a murder. In sum, he is a bladder blown up with wind, which the least flaw crushes to nothing.

16. A SERVING MAN

Is one of the makings up of a Gentleman, as well
as his clothes; and somewhat in the same nature,
for he is cast behind his master as fashionably as
his sword and his cloak are, and he is but *in querpo*
without him. His properness qualifies him, and of
that a good leg; for his head he has little use but to
keep it bare. A good dull wit best suits with him
to comprehend common sense and a trencher; for
any greater store of brain it makes him but tumul-
tuous, and seldom thrives with him. He follows his
master's steps, as well in conditions as the street:
if he wench or drink, he comes after in an under
kind and thinks it a part of his duty to be like him.
He is indeed wholly his master's; of his faction, of
his cut, of his pleasures. He is handsome for his
credit, and drunk for his credit; and if he have
power in the cellar, commands the parish. He is
one that keeps the best company and is none of it;
for he knows all the Gentlemen his master knows,
and picks from thence some hawking and horse-race
terms, which he swaggers with in the ale-house,
where he is only called master. His mirth is bawdy
jests with the wenches, and behind the door bawdy
earnest. The best work he does is his marrying, for
it makes an honest woman, and if he follows in it
his master's direction it is commonly the best
service he does him.

17. A TOO IDLY RESERVED MAN

Is one that is a fool with discretion: or a strange piece of politician, that manages the state of himself. His actions are his Privy Council, wherein no man must partake beside. He speaks under rule and prescription, and dare not shew his teeth without Machiavelli. He converses with his neighbours as he would in Spain, and fears an inquisitive man as much as the Inquisition. He suspects all questions for examinations, and thinks you would pick something out of him, and avoids you. His breast is like a Gentlewoman's closet, which locks up every toy and trifle, or some bragging mountebank, that makes every stinking thing a secret. He delivers you common matters with great conjuration of silence, and whispers you in the ear Acts of Parliament. You may as soon wrest a tooth from him as a paper, and whatsoever he reads is letters. He dares not talk of great men for fear of bad comments, and he "knows now how his words may be misapplied." Ask his opinion and he tells you his doubt: and he never hears anything more astonishedly than what he knows before. His words are like the cards at Primivist, where six is eighteen and seven one-and-twenty, for they never signify what they sound; but if he tell you he will do a thing it is as much as if he swore he would not. He is one indeed that takes all men to be craftier than they are, and puts himself to a great deal of affliction to hinder their plots and designs where they mean freely. He has been long a riddle himself, but at last finds Oedipusses; for his over-acted dissimulation discovers him, and men do with him as they would with Hebrew letters, spell him backwards, and read him.

18. A TAVERN

Is a degree, or (if you will) a pair of stairs above
an Alehouse, where men are drunk with more credit
and apology. If the Vintner's nose be at the door it
is a sign sufficient, but the absence of this is supplied
by the Ivy-bush. The rooms are ill breathed, like
the drinkers that have been washed well over-night,
and are smelt too fasting next morning; not furnished
with beds apt to be defiled, but more necessary
implements, stools, table, and a chamber-pot. It is
a broacher of more news than hogsheads, and more
jests than news, which are sucked up here by some
spongy brain, and from thence squeezed into a
Comedy. Men come here to make merry, but
indeed make a noise, and this music above is ans-
wered with the clinking below. The drawers are
the civillest people in it, men of good bringing up,
and howsoever we esteem of them, none can boast
more justly of their high calling. 'Tis the best
theatre of natures, where they are truly acted, not
played, and the business as in the rest of the world
up and down, to wit, from the bottom of the cellar
to the great chamber. A melancholy man would find
here matter to work upon, to see heads as brittle
as glasses, and often broken; men come hither to
quarrel, and come hither to make friends, and if
Plutarch will lend me his simile, it is even Telephus's
sword that makes wounds and cures them. It is
the common consumption of the afternoon, and the
murderer or maker away of a rainy day. It is the
Torrid Zone that scorches the face, and tobacco the
gun-powder that blows it up. Much harm would be
done, if the charitable vintner had not water ready
for these flames. A house of sin you may call it,
but not a house of darkness, for the candles are never

out, and it is like those countries far in the North where it is as clear at midnight as at mid-day. After a long sitting it becomes like a street in a dashing shower, where the spouts are flushing above and the conduits running below, while the Jordans like swelling rivers overflow their banks. To give you the total reckoning of it, it is the busy man's recreation, the idle man's business, the melancholy man's sanctuary, the stranger's welcome, the Inns-of-Court man's entertainment, the scholar's kindness, and the citizen's courtesy. It is the study of sparkling wits, and a cup of Sherry their book, where we leave them.

19. A SHARK

Is one whom all other means have failed, and he now lives of himself. He is some needy cashiered fellow, whom the world has oft flung off, yet still clasps again, and is like one a-drowning, fastens upon anything that's next at hand. Amongst other of his shipwrecks he has happily lost shame, and this want supplies him. No man puts his brain to more use than he, for his life is a daily invention and each meal a new stratagem. He has an excellent memory for his acquaintance ; though there passed but " how do you " betwixt them seven years ago, it shall suffice for an embrace, and that for money. He offers you a pottle of sack out of his joy to see you, and in requital of this courtesy you can do no less than pay for it. He is fumbling with his purse-strings,

as a school-boy with his points when he is going to
be whipped, till the master weary with long stay
forgives him. When the reckoning is paid, he says
"it must not be so," yet is straight pacified, and
cries, "what remedy?" His borrowings are like
subsidies, each man a shilling or two, as he can well
dispend, which they lend him, not with the hope to
be repaid but that he will come no more. He holds
a strange tyranny over men, for he is their debtor
and they fear him as a creditor. He is proud of
any employment though it be but to carry commendations, which he will be sure to deliver at eleven of
the clock. They in courtesy bid him stay, and he
in manners cannot deny them. If he find but a
good look to assure his welcome, he becomes their
half-boarder, and haunts the threshold so long till
he forces good natures to the necessity of a quarrel.
Public invitations he will not wrong with his absence,
and is the best witness of the Sheriff's hospitality.
Men shun him at length as they would an infection, and he is never crossed in his way if there be
but a lane to escape him. He has done with the age
as his clothes to him, hung on as long as he could,
and at last drops off.

20. AN INSOLENT MAN

Is a fellow newly great and newly proud: one that
hath put himself into another face upon his preferment, for his own was not bred to it. One whom
fortune hath shot up to some office of authority; and
he shoots up his neck to his fortune, and will not

bate you an inch of either. His very countenance and gesture bespeak how much he is, and if you understand him not, he tells you, and concludes every period with his place, which you must and shall know. He is one that looks on all men as if he were very angry, but especially on those of his acquaintance, whom he beats off with a surlier distance, as men apt to mistake him because they have known him. And for this cause he knows not you till you have told him your name, which " he thinks he has heard, but forgot," and with much ado seems to recover. If you have anything to use him in, you are his vassal for that time and must give him the patience of an injury, which he does only to shew what he may do. He snaps you up ditterly because he will be offended, and tells you you are saucy and troublesome, and sometimes takes your money in this language. His very courtesies are intolerable, they are done with such arrogance and imputation; and he is the only man you may hate after a good turn and not be ungrateful; and men reckon it among their calamities to be beholden unto him. No vice draws with it a more general hostility and makes men readier to search into his faults, and of them his beginning: and no tale so unlikely but is willingly heard of him and believed. And commonly such men are of no merit at all; but make out in pride what they want in worth, and fence themselves with a stately kind of behaviour from that contempt would pursue them. They are men whose preferment does us a great deal of wrong, and when they are down we may laugh at them without breach of good nature.

21. ACQUAINTANCE

Is the first draught of a friend, whom we must lay down oft thus, as the foul copy, before we can write him perfect and true; for from hence, as from a probation, men take a degree in our respect, till at last they wholly possess us. For acquaintance is the herd, and friendship the pair chosen out of it; by which at last we begin to appropriate, and enclose to ourselves, what before lay in common with others. And commonly where it grows not up to this, it falls as low as may be: and no poorer relation than old acquaintance, of whom we only ask how they do for fashion's sake, and care not. The ordinary use of acquaintance is but somewhat a more boldness of society, a sharing of talk, news, drink, mirth together: but sorrow is the right of a friend, as a thing nearer our heart, and to be delivered with it. Nothing easier than to create acquaintance: the mere being in company once, does it; whereas friendship like children is engendered by a more inward mixture and coupling together; when we are acquainted not with their virtues only, but their faults too, their passions, their fears, their shame, and are bold on both sides to make their discovery. And as it is in the love of the body, which is then at the height and full when it has power and admittance into the hidden and worst parts of it; so it is in friendship with the mind, when those *verenda* of the soul, and those things which we dare not shew the world, are bare and detected one to another. Some men are familiar with all, and those commonly friends to none; for friendship is a sullener thing, as a con-tracter and taker up of our affections to some few, and suffers them not loosely to be scattered on all men. The poorest tie of acquaintance is that of

place and country, which are shifted as the place,
and missed but while the fancy of that continues.
These are only then gladdest of other when they
meet in some foreign region, where the encompassing
of strangers unites them closer, till at last they get
new and throw off one another. Men of parts and
eminency, as their acquaintance is more sought for,
so they are generally more staunch of it, not out of
pride only, but fear to let too many in too near them:
for it is with men as with pictures, the best show
better afar off and at distance; and the closer you
come to them the coarser they are. The best
judgement of a man is taken from his acquaintance;
for friends and enemies are both partial, whereas
these see him truest because calmest, and are no
way so engaged to lie for him. And men that grow
strange after acquaintance seldom piece together
again, as those that have tasted meat and dislike it,
out of a mutual experience disrelishing one another.

22. A CARRIER

Is his own hackneyman; for he lets himself out
to travel as well as his horses. He is the ordinary
embassador between friend and friend, the father
and the son, and brings rich presents to the one, but
never returns any back again. He is no *unlettered*
man, though in show simple; for questionless, he
has much in his budget, which he can utter too in
fit time and place. He is the Vault in Gloucester

Church, that conveys whispers at a distance; for he takes the sound out of your mouth at York and makes it be heard as far as London. He is the young student's joy and expectation, and the most accepted guest, to whom they lend a willing hand to discharge him of his burden. His first greeting is commonly, " Your friends are well "; and to prove it, in a piece of Gold delivers their blessing. You would think him a churlish blunt fellow, but they find in him many tokens of humanity. He is a great afflicter of the high-ways and beats them out of measure, which injury is sometimes revenged by the purse-taker; and then the voyage miscarries. No man domineers more in his inn, nor calls his host unreverently with more presumption, and this arrogance proceeds out of the strength of his horses. He forgets not his load where he takes his ease, for he is drunk commonly before he goes to bed. He is like the prodigal child, still packing away, and still returning again. But let him pass.

23. A MERE COMPLIMENTAL MAN

Is one to be held off still at the same distance you are now; for you shall have him but thus, and if you enter on him further you lose him. Methinks Virgil well expresses him in those well-behaved ghosts that Aeneas met with, that were friends to talk with, and men to look on, but if he grasped them, but air. He is one that lies kindly to you, and for good fashion's sake, and 'tis discourtesy in you to believe him. His words are but so many fine phrases set together, which serve equally for all men, and are equally to no purpose. Each fresh encounter with a man puts him to the same part again, and he goes over to you what he said to him was last with him. He kisses your hands as he kissed his before, and " is your servant to be commanded," but you shall entreat of him nothing. His proffers are universal and general, with exceptions against all particulars. He will do anything for you: but if you urge him to this, he cannot, or to that, he is engaged: but he will do anything. Promises he accounts but a kind of mannerly words, and in the expectation of your manners not to exact them: if you do, he wonders at your ill breeding, that cannot distinguish betwixt what is spoken and what is meant. No man gives better satisfaction at the first, and comes off more with the eulogy of a kind Gentleman till you know him better, and then you know him for nothing. And commonly those most rail at him that have before most commended him. The best is, he cozens you in a fair manner and abuses you with great respect.

24. A POOR FIDDLER

Is a Man and a Fiddle out of case: and he in worse case than his fiddle. One that rubs two sticks together (as the Indians strike fire), and rubs a poor

living out of it; partly from this, and partly from
your charity, which is more in the hearing than giving
him, for he sells nothing dearer than to be gone.
He is just so many strings above a beggar, though he
have but two: and yet he begs too, only not in the
downright " for God's sake," but with a shrugging
" God bless you," and his face is more pined than
the blind man's. Hunger is the greatest pain he
takes, except a broken head sometimes, and the
labouring *John Dory*. Otherwise his life is so many
fits of mirth, and 'tis some mirth to see him. A
good feast shall draw him five miles by the nose, and
you shall track him again by the scent. His other
pilgrimages are fairs and good houses, where his
devotion is great to the Christmas; and no man
loves good times better. He is in league with the
tapsters for the worshipful of the inn, whom he
torments next morning with his art, and has their
names more perfect than their men. A new song
is better to him than a new jacket, especially if bawdy,
which he calls merry, and hates naturally the Puritan,
as an enemy to this mirth. A country wedding and
Whitsun ale are the two main places he domineers in,
where he goes for a musician, and overlooks the
bagpipe. The rest of him is drunk, and in the
stocks.

25. A YOUNG MAN

He is now out of nature's protection, though not
yet able to guide himself; but left loose to the world
and fortune, from which the weakness of his child-

hood preserved him; and now his strength exposes him. He is indeed just of age to be miserable, yet in his own conceit first begins to be happy; and he is happier in this imagination, and his misery not felt is less. He sees yet but the outside of the world and men, and conceives them according to their appearing glister, and out of this ignorance believes them. He pursues all vanities for happiness, and enjoys them best in this fancy. His reason serves not to curb, but understand his appetite, and prosecute the motions thereof with a more eager earnestness. Himself is his own temptation, and needs not Satan; and the World will come hereafter. He leaves repentance for gray hairs, and performs it in being covetous. He is mingled with the vices of the age as the fashion and custom, with which he longs to be acquainted, and sins to better his understanding. He conceives his youth as the season of his lust and the hour wherein he ought to be bad; and because he would not lose his time, spends it. He distastes religion as a sad thing, and is six years elder for a thought of heaven. He scorns and fears, and yet hopes for old age, but dare not imagine it with wrinkles. He loves and hates with the same inflammation, and when the heat is over is cool alike to friends and enemies. His friendship is seldom so steadfast but that lust, drink or anger may overturn it. He offers you his blood to-day in kindness, and is ready to take yours to-morrow. He does seldom anything which he wishes not to do again, and is only wise after a misfortune. He suffers much for his knowledge, and a great deal of folly it is makes him a wise man. He is free from many vices by being not grown to the performance, and is only more virtuous out of weakness. Every action is his danger, and every man his ambush. He is a ship without pilot or tackling, and only good fortune may steer him. If he scape this age, he has scaped a tempest, and may live to be a man.

26. AN OLD COLLEGE BUTLER

Is none of the worst students in the house, for he keeps the set hours at his book more duly than any. His authority is great over men's good names, which he charges many times with shrewd aspersions, which they hardly wipe off without payment. His box and counters prove him to be a man of reckoning; yet he is stricter in his accounts than a usurer, and delivers not a farthing without writing. He doubles the pains of Gallobelgicus, for his books go out once a quarter, and they are much in the same nature, brief notes and sums of affairs, and are out of request as soon. His comings in are like a tailor's, from the shreds of bread, the chippings, and remnants of the broken crust: excepting his vails from the barrel, which poor folks buy for their hogs but drink themselves. He divides a halfpenny loaf with more subtilty than Keckerman, and sub-divides the *à primo ortum* so nicely that a stomach of great capacity can hardly apprehend it. He is a very sober man considering his manifold temptations of drink and strangers, and if he be over-seen, 'tis within his own liberties and no man ought to take exception. He is never so well pleased with his place as when a Gentleman is beholden to him for showing him the buttery, whom he greets with a cup of single beer and sliced manchet, and tells him 'tis the fashion of the College. He domineers over Freshmen when they first come to the hatch, and puzzles them with strange language of *Cues* and *Cees*, and some broken Latin which he has learnt at his bin. His faculties extraordinary is the warming of a pair of cards and telling out a dozen of counters for Post and Pair, and no man is more methodical in these businesses. Thus he spends his age, till the tap of it is run out, and then a fresh one is set abroach.

27. A MEDDLING MAN

Is one that has nothing to do with his business, and yet no man busier than he, and his business is most in his face. He is one thrusts himself violently into all employments, unsent for, unfeed, and many times unthanked; and his part in it is only an eager bustling, that rather keeps ado than does anything. He will take you aside, and question you of your affair, and listen with both ears, and look earnestly; and then it is nothing so much yours as his. He snatches what you are doing out of your hands, and cries " Give it me," and does it worse, and lays an engagement upon you too, and you must thank him for his pains. He lays you down an hundred wild plots, all impossible things, which you must be ruled by perforce, and he delivers them with a serious and counselling forehead; and there is a great deal more wisdom in this forehead than his head. He will woo for you, solicit for you, and woo

you to suffer him; and scarce anything done, wherein
his letter, or his journey, or at least himself is not
seen: if he have no task in it else, he will rail yet on
some side, and is often beaten when he need not.
Such men never thoroughly weigh any business, but
are forward only to show their zeal, when many
times this forwardness spoils it, and then they cry
they have done what they can, that is as much hurt.
Wise men still deprecate these men's kindnesses, and
are beholden to them rather to let them alone; as
being one trouble more in all business, and which a
man shall be hardest rid of.

28. AN UPSTART COUNTRY KNIGHT

Is a Holiday Clown and differs only in the
stuff of his clothes, not the stuff of himself. His
honour was somewhat preposterous, for he bore the
King's sword before he had arms to wield it; yet
being once laid o'er the shoulder with a Knighthood,
he finds the Herald his friend. His father was a
man of good stock, though but a tanner or usurer;
he purchased the land, and his son the title. He
has doffed off the name of a Country Fellow, but the
look not so easy, and his face bears still a relish of
churn-milk. He is guarded with more gold lace
than all the gentlemen of the country, yet his body
makes his clothes still out of fashion. His house-
keeping is seen much in the distinct families of dogs,
and serving-men attendant on their kennels, and the

deepness of their throats is the depth of his discourse. A hawk he esteems the true burthen of Nobility, and is exceeding ambitious to seem delighted in the sport, and have his fist gloved with his Jesses. A Justice of Peace he is, to domineer in his parish and do his neighbour wrong with more right. And very scandalous he is in his authority, for no sin almost which he will not commit. He will be drunk with his hunters for company, and stain his gentility with droppings of ale. He is fearful of being Sheriff of the Shire by instinct, and dreads the Assize-week as much as the prisoner. In sum, he's but a clod of his own earth; or his land is the dunghill, and he the cock that crows over it. And commonly his race is quickly run and his children's children, though they scape hanging, return to the place from whence they came.

29. A GOOD OLD MAN

Is the best antiquity, and which we may with least vanity admire. One whom time hath been thus long a-working, and like winter fruit ripened when others are shaken down. He hath taken out as many lessons of the world as days, and learnt the best thing in it, the vanity of it. He looks over his former life as a danger well past, and would not hazard himself to begin again. His lust was long broken before his body, yet he is glad this temptation is broke too, and that he is fortified from it by this weakness. The next door of death sads him not, but he expects it calmly as his turn in nature; and fears more his recoiling back to childishness than dust. All men look on him as a common father, and on old age for his sake as a reverent thing. His very presence and face puts vice out of countenance, and makes it an indecorum in a vicious man. He practises his experience on youth without the harshness of reproof, and in his counsel is good company. He has some old stories still of his own seeing to confirm what he says, and makes them better in the telling; yet is not troublesome neither with the same tale again, but remembers with them how oft he has told them. His old sayings and morals seem proper to his beard; and the poetry of Cato does well out of his mouth, and he speaks it as if he were the author. He is not apt to put the boy on a younger man, nor the fool on a boy; but can distinguish gravity from a sour look, and the less testy he is, the more regarded. You must pardon him if he like his own times better than these, because those things are follies to him now that were wisdom then; yet he makes us of that opinion too, when we see him and conjecture those times by so good a relic. He is a man capable of a dearness with the youngest men; yet he not youthfuller for them, but they older for him; and no man credits more his acquaintance. He goes away at last, too soon whensoever, with all men's sorrow but his own; and his memory is fresh when it is twice as old.

30. AN IDLE GALLANT

Is one that was born and shaped for his clothes:
and if Adam had not fallen, had lived to no purpose.
He gratulates therefore the first sin, and fig leaves
that were an occasion of bravery. His first care is
his dress, the next his body, and in the uniting of
these two lies his soul and its faculties. He observes
London trulier than the Terms, and his business is
the street, the Stage, the Court, and those places
where a proper man is best shown. If he be qualified
in gaming extraordinary, he is so much the more
gentle and complete, and he learns the best oaths for
the purpose. These are a great part of his discourse,
and he is as curious in their newness as the fashion.
His other talk is ladies and such pretty things, or
some jest at a play. His pick-tooth bears a great
part in his discourse; so does his body, the upper
parts whereof are as starched as his linen, and
perchance use the same laundress. He has learnt
to ruffle his face from his boot, and takes great
delight in his walk to hear his spurs jingle. Though
his life pass somewhat slidingly, yet he seems very
careful of the time, for he is still drawing his watch
out of his pocket, and spends part of his hours in
numbering them. He is one never serious but with
his tailor, when he is in conspiracy for the next
device. He is furnished with his jests, as some
wanderer with sermons, some three for all congregations, one especially against the scholar, a man to
him much ridiculous, whom he knows by no other
definition but " a silly fellow in black." He is a
kind of walking Mercer's Shop, and shews you one
stuff to-day and another to-morrow, an ornament to
the rooms he comes in, as the fair bed and hangings
be; and is merely ratable accordingly, fifty or an

hundred pound as his suit is. His main ambition
is to get a Knighthood, and then an old lady, which
if he be happy in, he fills the stage and a coach so
much longer. Otherwise, himself and his clothes
grow stale together, and he is buried commonly ere
he dies, in the Gaol or the Country.

31. A CONSTABLE

Is a Viceroy in the street, and no man stands more
upon 't that he is the King's Officer. His juris-
diction extends to the next stocks, where he has
commission for the heels only, and sets the rest of
the body at liberty. He is scarecrow to that Ale-
house where he drinks not his morning draught, and
apprehends a drunkard for not standing in the King's
name. Beggars fear him more than the Justice and
as much as the whipstock, whom he delivers over
to his subordinate magistrates, the Bridewell-man
and the Beadle. He is a great stickler in the tumults
of double jugs, and ventures his head by his place,
which is broke many times to keep whole the peace.
He is never so much in his majesty as in his night-
watch, where he sits in his chair of state, a shop-stall,
and environed with a guard of halberts, examines all
passengers. He is a very careful man in his Office,
but if he stay up after midnight you shall take him
napping.

32. A FLATTERER

Is the picture of a friend, and as pictures flatter many times, so he oft shews fairer than the true substance. His look, conversation, company, and all the outwardness of friendship more pleasing by odds, for a true friend dare take the liberty to be sometimes offensive, whereas he is a great deal more cowardly and will not let the least hold go for fear of losing you. Your mere sour look affrights him, and makes him doubt his cashiering. And this is one sure mark of him, that he is never first angry, but ready though upon his own wrong to make satisfaction. Therefore he is never yoked upon a poor man, or any that stands on the lower ground, but whose fortunes may tempt his pains to deceive him. Him he learns first, and learns well, and grows perfecter in his humours than himself, and by this door enters upon his soul; of which he is able at last to take the very print and mark, and fashion his own by it, like a false key to open all your secrets. All his affections jump even with yours: he is beforehand with your thoughts, and able to suggest them unto you. He will commend to you first what he knows you like, and has always some absurd story or other of your enemy, and then wonders how your two opinions should jump in that man. He will ask your counsel sometimes as a man of deep judgement, and has a secret of purpose to disclose you, and whatsoever you say is persuaded. He listens to your words with great attention, and sometimes will object that you may confute him, and then protests he never heard so much before. A piece of wit bursts him with an overflowing laughter, and he remembers it for you to all companies, and laughs again in the telling. He is one never chides you but for your virtues, as,

" You are too good," " too honest," " too religious " ;
when his chiding may seem but the earnester commendation, and yet would fain chide you out of them
too; for your vice is the thing he has use of, and
wherein you may best use him, and he is never more
active than in the worst diligences. Thus at last he
possesses you from yourself, and then expects but
his hire to betray you. And it is a happiness not
to discover him; for as long as you are happy, you
shall not.

33. A DOWNRIGHT SCHOLAR

Is one that has much learning in the ore, un-
wrought and untried, which time and experience
fashions and refines. He is good metal in the inside,
though rough and unscoured without, and therefore
hated of the courtier, that is quite contrary. The
time has got a vein of making him ridiculous, and
men laugh at him by tradition, and no unlucky
absurdity but is put upon his profession and
" done like a scholar." But his fault is only this,
that his mind is somewhat too much taken up with
his mind, and his thoughts not loaden with any
carriage besides. He has not put on the quaint garb
of the age, which is now become a man's *Imprimis*
and all the *Item*. He has not humbled his meditations to the industry of compliment, not afflicted his
brain in an elaborate leg. His body is not set upon
nice pins, to be turning and flexible for every motion,
but his scrape is homely, and his nod worse. He

cannot kiss his hand and cry " Madame," nor talk idly enough to bear her company. His smacking of a gentlewoman is somewhat too savoury, and he mistakes her nose for her lips. A very woodcock would puzzle him in carving, and he wants the logic of a capon. He has not the glib faculty of sliding over a tale, but his words come squeamishly out of his mouth, and the laughter commonly before the jest. He names this word " College " too often, and his discourse beats too much on the University. The perplexity of mannerliness will not let him feed, and he is sharp set at an argument when he should cut his meat. He is discarded for a gamester at all games but one-and-thirty, and at tables he reaches not beyond doublets. His fingers are not long and drawn out to handle a fiddle, but his fist is clenched with the habit of disputing. He ascends a horse somewhat sinisterly, though not on the left side, and they both go jogging in grief together. He is exceedingly censured by the Inns-o'-Court men for that heinous vice being out of fashion. He cannot speak to a dog in its own dialect, and understands Greek better than the language of a falconer. He has been used to a dark room and dark clothes, and his eyes dazzle at a satin suit. The hermitage of his study has made him somewhat uncouth in the world, and men make him worse by staring on him. Thus is he silly and ridiculous, and it continues with him for some quarter of a year out of the University. But practise him a little in men, and brush him over with good company, and he shall out-balance those glisterers as much as a solid substance does a feather, or gold gold-lace.

34. A HIGH-SPIRITED MAN

Is one that looks like a proud man, but is not: you may forgive him his looks for his worth's sake, for they are only too proud to be base. One whom no rate can buy off from the least piece of his freedom, and make him digest an unworthy thought an hour. He cannot crouch to a great man to possess him, nor fall low on the earth to rebound never so high again. He stands taller on his own bottom, than others on the advantage ground of fortune, as having solidly that honour of which title is but the pomp. He does homage to no man for his great stile's sake, but is strictly just in the exaction of respect again, and will not bate you a compliment. He is more sensible of a neglect than an undoing, and scorns no man so much as his surly threatener. A man quickly fired, and quickly laid down with satisfaction, but remits any injury sooner than words. Only to himself he is irreconcileable, whom he never forgives a disgrace, but is still stabbing himself with the thought of it, and no disease that he dies of sooner. He is one had rather perish than be beholden for his life, and strives more to be quit with his friend than his enemy. Fortune may kill him but not deject him, nor make him fall into a humbler key than before, but he is now loftier than ever in his own defence; you shall hear him talk still after thousands, and he becomes it better than those that have it. One that is above the world and its drudgery, and cannot pull down his thoughts to the pelting businesses of life. He would sooner accept the gallows than a mean trade, or anything that might disparage the height of man in him, and yet thinks no death comparably base to hanging neither. One that will do nothing upon command, though he would do it otherwise:

and if ever he does evil, it is when he is dared to it. He is one that if fortune equal his worth puts a luster in all preferment; but if otherwise he be too much crossed, turns desperately melancholy, and scorns mankind.

35. A PLAIN COUNTRY FELLOW

Is one that manures his ground well, but lets himself lie fallow and untilled. He has reason enough to do his business, and not enough to be idle or melancholy. He seems to have the punishment of Nebuchadnezzar, for his conversation is among beasts, and his talons none of the shortest, only he eats not grass, because he loves not sallets. His hand guides the plough, and the plough his thoughts, and his ditch and landmark is the very mound of his meditations. He expostulates with his oxen very understandingly, and speaks " Gee " and " Ree " better than English His mind is not much distracted with objects; but if a good fat cow come in his way he stands dumb and astonished, and though his haste be never so great will fix here half-an-hour's contemplation. His habitation is some poor thatched roof, distinguished from his barn by the loop-holes that let out smoke, which the rain had long since washed through but for the double ceiling of bacon on the inside, which has hung there from his grandsire's time, and is yet to make rashers for posterity. His dinner is his other work, for he sweats at it as much as at his labour; he is a terrible fastener on a piece of beef, and you may hope to stave the Guard off sooner. His religion is a part of his copy-hold, which he takes from his landlord, and refers it wholly to his discretion. Yet if he give him leave, he is a good Christian to his power, that is comes to church in his best clothes, and sits there with his neighbours, where he is capable only of two prayers, for rain and fair weather. He apprehends God's blessings only in a good year or a fat pasture, and never praises Him but on *good ground*. Sunday he esteems a day to make merry in, and thinks a bag-pipe as essential to it as Evening Prayer, where he walks very solemnly after service with his hands coupled behind him, and censures the dancing of his parish. His compliment with his neighbour is a good thump on the back, and his salutation commonly some blunt curse. He thinks nothing to be vices but pride and ill husbandry, from which he will gravely dissuade the youth and has some thrifty hobnail proverbs to clout his discourse. He is a niggard all the week except only market-day, where if his corn sell well, he thinks he may be drunk with a good conscience. His feet never stinks so unbecomingly as when he trots after a lawyer in Westminster-Hall, and even cleave the ground with hard scraping in beseeching his Worship to take his money. He is sensible of no calamity but the burning of a stack of corn or the overflowing of a meadow, and thinks Noah's flood the greatest plague that ever was, not because it drowned the world, but spoiled the grass. For death he is never troubled, and if he get in but his harvest before, let it come when it will, he cares not.

36. A MERE GULL CITIZEN

Is one much about the same model and pitch of brain that the Clown is, only of somewhat a more polite and finical ignorance, and as sillily scorns him as he is sillily admired by him. The quality of the city hath afforded him some better dress of clothes and language, which he uses to the best advantage, and is so much the more ridiculous. His chief education is the visits of his shop, where if courtiers and fine ladies resort, he is infected with so much more eloquence, and if he catches one word extraordinary, wears it for ever. You shall hear him mince a compliment sometimes that was never made for him; and no man pays dearer for good words, for he is oft payed with them. He is suited rather fine than in the fashion, and has still something to distinguish him from a gentleman, though his doublet cost more; especially on Sundays, bride-groom-like, where he carries the state of a very solemn man, and keeps his pew as his shop; and it is a great part of his devotion to feast the minister. But his chiefest guest is a customer, which is the greatest relation he acknowledges, especially if you be an honest gentleman, that is, trust him to cozen you enough. His friendships are a kind of gossiping friendships, and those commonly within the circle of his trade, wherein he is careful principally to avoid two things, that is, poor men and suretyships. He is a man will spend his sixpence with a great deal of imputation, and no man makes more of a pint of wine than he. He is one bears a pretty kind of foolish love to scholars, and to Cambridge especially, for Stourbridge Fair's sake; and of these all are truants to him that are not preachers, and of these the loudest the best; and he is much ravished with the noise of a rolling tongue. He loves to hear discourses out of his element, and the less he understands the better pleased, which he expresses in a smile and some fond protestation. One that does nothing without his chuck, that is, his wife, with whom he is billing still in conspiracy, and the wantoner she is the more power she has over him; and she never stoops so low after him, but is the only woman goes better off a widow than a maid. In the education of his child no man fearfuller, and the danger he fears is a harsh schoolmaster, to whom he is alleging still the weakness of the boy, and pays a fine extraordinary for his mercy. The first whipping rids him to the University, and from thence rids him again for fear of starving, and the best he makes of him is some gull in plush. He is one loves to hear the famous acts of citizens, whereof the gilding of the Cross he counts the glory of this age; and the *Four Prentices of London* above all the Nine Worthies. He entitles himself to all the merits of his Company, whether schools, hospitals, or exhibitions, in which he is joint benefactor, though four hundred years ago, and upbraids them far more than those that gave them. Yet with all this folly he has wit enough to get wealth, and in that a sufficienter man than he that is wiser.

37. A LASCIVIOUS MAN

Is the servant he says of many mistresses, but all are but his lust: to which only he is faithful and none besides, and spends his best blood and spirits in the service. His soul is the bawd to his body, and those that assist him in this nature the nearest to it. No man abuses more the name of love, or those whom he applies this name to; for his love is like his stomach to feed on what he loves, and the end of it to surfeit and loath, till a fresh appetite rekindle him; and it kindles on any sooner than who deserve best of him. There is a great deal of malignity in this vice, for it loves still to spoil the best things, and a virgin often rather than beauty, because the undoing here is greater, and consequently his glory. No man laughs more at his sin than he, or is so extremely tickled with the remembrance of it; and he is more violent to a modest ear than to her he deflowered. A bawdy jest enters deep into him, and whatsoever you speak he will draw to bawdry, and his wit is never so good as here. His unchastest part is his tongue, for that commits always what he must act seldomer and that commits with all which he acts with few; for he is his own worst reporter, and men believe as bad of him, and yet do not believe him. Nothing harder to his persuasion than a chaste man, no eunuch, and makes a scoffing miracle at it if you tell him of a maid. And from this mistrust it is that such men fear marriage, or at least marry such as are of bodies to be trusted, to whom they sell that lust which they buy of others, and make their wife a revenue to their mistress. They are men not easily reformed, because they are so little ill-persuaded of their illness, and have such pleas from man and nature. Besides it is a jeering and flouting vice, and apt to put jests on the reprover. The pox only converts them, and that only when it kills them.

38. A PLAYER

He knows the right use of the world, wherein he comes to play a part and so away. His life is not idle, for it is all action, and no man need be more wary in his doings, for the eyes of all men are upon him. His profession has in it a kind of contradiction, for none is more disliked, and yet none more applauded, and he has this misfortune of some scholars, too much wit makes him a fool. He is like our painting gentlewomen, seldom in his own face, seldomer in his clothes; and he pleases the better he counterfeits, except only when he is disguised with straw for gold-lace. He does not only personate on the stage, but sometimes in the street, for he is masked still in the habit of a gentleman. His parts find him oaths and good words, which he keeps for his use and discourse, and makes shew with them of a fashionable companion. He is tragical on the stage, but rampant in the tiring-house, and swears oaths there which he never conned. The waiting-women spectators are over-ears in love with him, and ladies send for him to act in their chambers. Your Inns-of-Court men were undone but for him, he is their chief guest and employment, and the sole business that makes them afternoon's-men. The Poet only is his tyrant, and he is bound to make his friend's friend drunk at his charge. Shrove-Tuesday he fears as much as the bawds, and Lent is more damage to him than the butcher. He was never so much discredited as in one act, and that was of Parliament, which gives hostlers privileges before him, for which he abhors it more than a corrupt Judge. But to give him his due, one well-furnished actor has enough in him for five common gentlemen, and if he have a good body, for six; and for resolution he shall challenge any Cato, for it has been his practice to die bravely.

39. A DETRACTOR

Is one of more cunning and active envy, wherewith he gnaws not foolishly himself, but throws it abroad and would have it blister others. He is commonly some weak parted fellow, and worse minded, yet is strangely ambitious to match others, not by mounting their worth but bringing them down with his tongue to his own poorness. He is indeed like the red dragon that pursued the woman, for when he cannot over-reach another he opens his mouth and throws a flood after to drown him. You cannot anger him worse than to do well, and he hates you more bitterly for this than if you had cheated him of his patrimony with your own discredit. He is always slighting the general opinion, and wondering why such and such men should be applauded. Commend a good Divine, he cries " Postilling "; a Philologer, " Pedantry "; a Poet, " Rhyming "; a Schoolman, " dull wrangling "; a sharp conceit, " boyishness "; an honest man, " plausibility." He comes to public things not to learn but to catch, and if there be but one solecism that's all he carries away. He looks on all things with a prepared sourness, and is still furnished with a " Pish " beforehand, or some musty proverb that disrelishes all things whatsoever. If fear of the company make him second a commendation, it is like a law-writ, always with a clause of exception, or to smooth his way to some greater scandal. He will grant you something, and bate more; and this bating shall in conclusion take away all he granted. His speech concludes still with an " Oh but," and " I could wish one thing amended; " and this one thing shall be enough to deface all his former commendations. He will be very inward with a man to fish some bad out of him, and make his slanders hereafter more authentic when it is said " a friend reported it." He will inveigle you to naughtiness to get your good name into his clutches, and make you drunk to shew you reeling. He passes the more plausibly because all men have a smatch of his humour, and it is thought freeness which is malice. If he can say nothing of a man he will seem to speak riddles, as if he could tell strange stories if he would; and when he has racked his invention to the uttermost, he ends: " But I wish him well, and therefore must hold my peace." He is always listening and enquiring after men, and suffers not a cloak to pass by him unexamined. In brief, he is one that has lost all good himself, and is loth to find it in another.

40. A RASH MAN

Is a man too quick for himself: one whose actions put a leg still before his judgement, and out-run it. Every hot fancy or passion is the signal that sets him forward, and his reason comes still in the rear. One that has brain enough, but not patience to digest a business and stay the leisure of a second thought. All deliberation is to him a kind of sloth and freezing of action, and it shall burn him rather than take cold. He is always resolved at first thinking, and the ground he goes upon is " hap what may." Thus he enters not, but throws himself violently upon all things, and for the most part is as violently thrown off again: and as an obstinate " I will " was the preface to his undertaking, so his conclusion is commonly " I would I had not "; for such men seldom do anything that they are not forced to take in pieces again, and are so much further off from doing it, as they have done already. His friends are with him as his physician; sought to only in his sickness and extremity, and to help him out of that mire he has plunged himself into; for in the suddenness of his passions he would hear nothing, and now his ill success has allayed him he hears too late. He is a man still swayed with the first reports, and no man more in the power of a pick-thank than he. He is one will fight first, and then expostulate; condemn first, and then examine. He loses his friend in a fit of quarrelling, and in a fit of kindness undoes himself; and then curses the occasion drew this mischief upon him, and cries God mercy for it, and curses again. His repentance is merely a rage against himself, and he does something in itself to be repented again. He is a man whom fortune must go against much to make him happy, for had he been suffered his own way he had been undone.

41. A MERE YOUNG GENTLEMAN OF THE UNIVERSITY

Is one that comes there to wear a gown, and to say hereafter, he has been at the University. His father sent him thither because he heard there were the best fencing and dancing schools; from these he has his education, from his tutor the oversight. The first element of his knowledge is to be shown the colleges, and initiated in a tavern by the way, which hereafter he will learn of himself. The two marks of his seniority is the bare velvet of his gown and his proficiency at tennis, where when he can once play a set he is a Freshman no more. His study has commonly handsome shelves, his books neat silk strings, which he shews to his father's man, and is loth to untie or take down for fear of misplacing. Upon foul days for recreation he retires thither, and looks over the pretty book his tutor reads to him, which is commonly some short history, or a piece of Euphormio; for which his tutor gives him money to spend next day. His main loitering is at the Library, where he studies arms and books of honour, and turns a gentleman-critic in pedigrees. Of all things he endures not to be mistaken for a scholar, and hates a black suit though it be made of satin. His company is ordinarily some stale fellow, that has been notorious for an ingle to gold hatbands, whom he admires at first, afterwards scorns. If he have spirit or wit, he may light of better company and may learn some flashes of wit, which may do him knight's service in the country hereafter. But he is now gone to the Inns-of-Court, where he studies to forget what he learned before, his acquaintance and the fashion.

42. A WEAK MAN

Is a child at man's estate, one whom nature huddled up in haste, and left his best part unfinished. The rest of him is grown to be a man, only his brain stays behind. He is one that has not improved his first rudiments, nor attained any proficiency by his stay in the world: but we may speak of him yet as when he was in the bud, a good harmless nature, a well meaning mind and no more. It is his misery that he now most wants a tutor, and is too old to have one. He is two steps above a fool, and a great many more below a wise man: yet the fool is oft given him, and by those whom he esteems most. Some tokens of him are: He loves men better upon relation than experience, for he is exceedingly enamoured of strangers, and none quicklier a-weary of his friends. He charges you at a first meeting with all his secrets, and on better acquaintance grows more reserved. Indeed he is one that mistakes much his abusers for friends, and his friends for enemies, and he apprehends your hate in nothing so much as in good counsel. One that is flexible with anything but reason, and then only perverse; and you may better entice than persuade him. A servant to every tale and flatterer, and whom the last man still works over. A great affecter of wits and such prettinesses; and his company is costly to him, for he seldom has it but invited. His friendship commonly is begun in a supper and lost in lending money. The tavern is a dangerous place to him, for to drink and to be drunk is with him all one, and his brain is sooner quenched than his thirst He is drawn into naughtiness with company, but suffers alone, and the bastard commonly laid to his charge. One that will be patiently abused, and take exception a month after when he understands it, and then be abused again into a reconcilement; and you cannot endear him more than by cozening him, and it is a temptation to those that would not. One discoverable in all sillinesses to all men but himself, and you may take any man's knowledge of him better than his own. He will promise the same thing to twenty, and rather than deny one break with all. One that has no power over himself, over his business, over his friends, but a prey and pity to all; and if his fortunes once sink, men quickly cry " Alas " and forget him.

43. A TOBACCO-SELLER

Is the only man that finds good in it which others brag of, but do not; for it is meat, drink, and clothes to him. No man opens his ware with greater seriousness, or challenges your judgement more in the approbation. His shop is the rendezvous of spitting, where men dialogue with their noses, and their communication is smoke. It is the place only where Spain is commended, and preferred before England itself. He should be well experienced in the world, for he has daily trial of men's nostrils, and none is better acquainted with humours. He is the piecing commonly of some other trade, which is bawd to his Tobacco, and that to his wife, which is the flame that follows this smoke.

44. AN AFFECTED MAN

Is an extraordinary man in ordinary things. One that would go a strain beyond himself, and is taken in it. A man that overdoes all things with great solemnity of circumstance; and whereas with more negligence he might pass better, makes himself, with a great deal of endeavour, ridiculous. The fancy of some odd quaintnesses have put him clean beside his nature; he cannot be that he would, and hath lost what he was. He is one must be point-blank in every trifle, as if his credit and opinion hung upon it: the very space of his arms in an embrace studied before and premeditated; and the figure of his countenance of a fortnight's contriving. He will not curse you without book and *extempore*, but in some choice way, and perhaps as some great man curses. Every action of his cries " Do ye mark me ? " and men do mark him how absurd he is: for affectation is the most betraying humour, and nothing that puzzles a man less to find out than this. All the actions of his life are like so many things bodged in without any natural cadence or connection at all. You shall track him all through like a schoolboy's theme, one piece from one author and this from another, and join all in this general, that they are none of his own. You shall observe his mouth not made for that tone, nor his face for that simper; and it is his luck that his finest things most misbecome him. If he affect the Gentleman, as the humour most commonly lies that way, not the least punctilio of a fine man but he is strict in to a hair, even to their very negligences, which he cons as rules. He will not carry a knife with him to wound reputation; and pay double a reckoning rather than ignobly question it. And he is full of this " Ignobly " and " Nobly " and " Genteelly " and this mere fear to trespass against the Genteel way puts him out most of all. It is a humour runs through many things besides, but is an ill-favoured ostentation in all, and thrives not. And the best use of such men is, they are good parts in a play.

45. A POT-POET

Is the dregs of wit; yet mingled with good drink may have some relish. His inspirations are more real than others'; for they do but feign a God, but he has his by him. His verses run like the tap, and his invention as the barrel ebbs and flows at the mercy of the spigot. In thin drink he aspires not above a ballad, but a cup of sack inflames him and sets his muse and nose afire together. The Press is his Mint, and stamps him now and then a sixpence or two in reward of the baser coin his pamphlet. His works would scarce sell for three half-pence, though they are given oft for three shillings, but for the pretty title that allures the country Gentleman: and for which the printer maintains him in ale a fortnight. His verses are like his clothes, miserable centos and patches, yet their pace is not altogether so hobbling as an Almanac's. The death of a great man or the burning of a house furnish him with an argument, and the Nine Muses are out straight in mourning gown, and Melpomene cries " Fire, Fire." His other poems are but briefs in rhyme, and like the poor Greeks' collection to redeem from captivity. He is a man now much employed in commendations of our Navy, and a bitter inveigher against the Spaniard. His frequentest works go out in single sheets, and are chanted from market to market, to a vile tune and a worse throat; whilst the poor country wench melts like her butter to hear them. And these are the stories of some men of Tyburne, or a strange monster out of Germany: or sitting in a bawdy-house, he writes God's judgements. He ends at last in some obscure painted cloth, to which himself made the verses, and his life like a can too full spills upon the bench. He leaves twenty shillings on the score, which my Hostess loses.

46. A PLAUSIBLE MAN

Is one that would fain run an even path in the world and jut against no man. His endeavour is not to offend, and his aim the general opinion. His conversation is a kind of continued compliment, and his life a practice of manners. The relation he bears to others a kind of fashionable respect, not friendship but friendliness, which is equal to all and general, and his kindnesses seldom exceed courtesies. He loves not deeper mutualities, because he would not take sides nor hazard himself on displeasures, which he principally avoids. At your first acquaintance with him he is exceeding kind and friendly, and at your twentieth meeting after but friendly still.

He has an excellent command over his patience and
tongue, especially the last, which he accommodates
always to the times and persons, and speaks seldom
what is sincere, but what is civil. He is one that
uses all companies, drinks all healths, and is reasonable cool in all religions. He considers who are
friendly to the company, and speaks well where he
is sure to hear of it again. He can listen to a foolish
discourse with an applausive attention, and conceal
his laughter at nonsense. Silly men much honour
and esteem him, because by his fair reasoning with
them as with men of understanding he puts them
into an erroneous opinion of themselves, and makes
them forwarder hereafter to their own discovery.
He is one rather well thought on than beloved, and
that love he has is more of whole companies together
than any one in particular. Men gratify him
notwithstanding with a good report, and whatever
vices he has besides, yet having no enemies, he is
sure to be an honest fellow.

47. A BOWL-ALLEY

Is the place where there are three things thrown
away besides bowls, to wit, time, money and curses,
and the last ten for one. The best sport in it is the
gamesters, and he enjoys it that looks on and bets not.
It is the school of wrangling, and worse than the
schools, for men will cavil here for an hair's breadth,
and make a stir where a straw would end the controversy. No antic screws men's bodies into such

strange flexures, and you would think them here senseless, to speak sense to their bowl and put their trust in entreaties for a good cast. The betters are the factious noise of the alley, or the gamesters' beadsmen that pray for them. They are somewhat like those that are cheated by great men, for they lose their money and must say nothing. It is the best discovery of humours, especially in the losers, where you have fine variety of impatience, whilst some fret, some rail, some swear, and others more ridiculously comfort themselves with philosophy. To give you the moral of it; it is the emblem of the world, or the world's ambition: where most are short, or over, or wide or wrong-biased, and some few justle in to the Mistress, Fortune. And it is here as in the Court, where the nearest are most spited, and all blows aimed at the Toucher.

48. THE WORLD'S WISE MAN

Is an able and sufficient wicked man. It is a proof of his sufficiency that he is not called wicked, but wise. A man wholly determined in himself and his own ends, and his instruments herein anything that will do it. His friends are a part of his engines, and as they serve to his works, used or laid by. Indeed he knows not this thing of friend, but if he give you the name it is a sign he has a plot on you. Never more active in his businesses than when they are mixed with some harm to others; and 'tis his best play in this game to strike off and lie in the place. Successful commonly in these undertakings because he passes smoothly those rubs which others stumble at, as conscience and the like; and gratulates himself much in this advantage. Oaths and falsehood he counts the nearest way, and loves not by any means to go about. He has many fine quips at this folly of plain dealing, but his " tush " is greatest at religion; yet he uses this too, and virtue and good words, but is less dangerously a Devil than a Saint. He ascribes all honesty to an unpractisedness in the world, and conscience a thing merely for children. He scorns all that are so silly to trust him, and only not scorns his enemy, especially if as bad as himself. He fears him as a man well armed and provided, but sets boldly on good natures, as the most vanquishable. One that seriously admires those worst Princes, as Sforza, Borgia, and Richard the Third; and calls matters of deep villainy " things of difficulty." To whom murders are but " resolute acts," and treason " a business of great consequence." One whom two or three countries make up to this completeness, and he has travelled for the purpose. His deepest endearment is a communication of mischief, and then only you have him fast. His conclusion is commonly one of these two, either a great man, or hanged.

49. A SURGEON

Is one that has some business about this building or little house of man, whereof Nature is as it were the tiler, and he the plasterer. It is ofter out of reparations than an old parsonage, and then he is set on work to patch it again. He deals most with broken commodities, as a broken head, or a mangled face, and his gains are very ill got, for he lives by the hurts of the commonwealth. He differs from a physician as a sore does from a disease, or the sick from those that are not whole; the one distempers you within, the other blisters you without. He complains of the decay of valour in these days, and sighs for that slashing age of sword and buckler; and thinks the law against duels was made merely to wound his vocation. He had been long since undone if the charity of the stews had not relieved him, from whom he has his tribute as duly as the Pope; or a windfall sometimes from a tavern, if a quart pot hit right. The rareness of his custom makes him pitiless when it comes, and he holds a patient longer than our courts a cause. He tells you what danger you had been in if he had stayed but a minute longer, and though it be but a pricked finger he makes of it much matter. He is a reasonable cleanly man considering the scabs he has to deal with, and your finest ladies now and then are beholden to him for their best dressings. He curses old gentlewomen and their charity that makes his trade their alms; but his envy is never stirred so much as when gentlemen go over to fight upon Calais Sands, whom he wishes drowned ere they come there, rather than the French shall get his custom.

50. A PROPHANE MAN

Is one that denies God as far as the law gives him leave, that is, only does not say so in downright terms, for so far he may go. A man that does the greatest sins calmly and as the ordinary actions of life, and as calmly discourses of it again. He will tell you his business is to break such a Commandment, and the breaking of the Commandment shall tempt him to it. His words are but so many vomitings cast up to the loathsomeness of the hearers, only those of his company loathe it not. He will take upon him with oaths to pelt some tenderer man out of his company, and makes good sport at his conquest over the Puritan fool. The Scripture supplies him for jests, and he reads it of purpose to be thus merry. He will prove you his sin out of the Bible, and then ask if you will not take that authority. He never sees the Church but of purpose to sleep in it; or when some silly man preaches with whom he means to make sport, and is most jocund in the Church. One that nicknames Clergymen with all the terms of reproach, as *Rat*, *Blackcoat*, and the like, which he will be sure to keep up, and never calls them by other. That sings Psalms when he is drunk, and cries " God mercy " in mockery; for he must do it. He is one seems to dare God in all his actions, but indeed would out-dare the opinion of him, which would else turn him desperate; for Atheism is the refuge of such sinners, whose repentance would be only to hang themselves.

51. A CONTEMPLATIVE MAN

Is a scholar in this great University the world; and the same his book and study. He cloisters not his meditations in the narrow darkness of a room, but sends them abroad with his eyes, and his brain travels with his feet. He looks upon man from a high tower, and sees him trulier at this distance in his infirmities and poorness. He scorns to mix himself in men's actions, as he would to act upon a stage; but sits aloft on the scaffold a censuring spectator. He will not lose his time by being busy, or make so poor a use of the world as to hug and embrace it. Nature admits him as a partaker of her sports, and asks his approbation as it were of her own works and variety. He comes not in company because he would not be solitary, but finds discourse enough with himself, and his own thoughts are his excellent play-fellows. He looks not upon a thing as a yawning stranger at novelties; but his search is more mysterious and inward, and he spells Heaven out of Earth. He knits his observations together, and makes a ladder of them all to climb to God. He is free from vice because he has no occasion to employ it, and is above those ends that make men wicked. He has learnt all can here be taught him, and comes now to heaven to see more.

52. A SHE PRECISE HYPOCRITE

Is one in whom good women suffer, and have their truth misinterpreted by her folly. She is one, she knows not what herself if you ask her, but she is indeed one that has taken a toy at the fashion of religion, and is enamoured of the new-fangle. She

is a Nonconformist in a close stomacher and ruffle of
Geneva print, and her purity consists much in her
linen. She has heard of the Rag of Rome, and
thinks it a very sluttish religion, and rails at the
Whore of Babylon for a very naughty woman.
She has left her virginity as a relic of Popery, and
marries in her tribe without a ring. Her devotion
at Church is much in the turning up of her eye, and
turning down the leaf in her book when she hears
named chapter and verse. When she comes home
she commends the sermon for the scripture, and two
hours. She loves preaching better than praying, and
of preachers Lecturers, and thinks the weekday's
exercise far more edifying than the Sunday's. Her
oftest gossipings are Sabbath-days' journeys, where
(though an enemy to superstition) she will go in
pilgrimage five miles to a silenced minister, when
there is a better sermon in her own parish. She
doubts of the Virgin Mary's salvation, and dare not
saint her, but knows her own place in heaven as
perfectly as the pew she has a key to. She is so
taken up with Faith she has no room for Charity,
and understands no good works but what are wrought
on the sampler. She accounts nothing vices but
superstition and an oath, and thinks adultery a less
sin than to swear " by my truly." She rails at
other women by the names of Jezebel and Delilah;
and calls her own daughters Rebecca and Abigail,
and not Anne but Hannah. She suffers them
not to learn on the virginals because of their
affinity with organs, but is reconciled to the bells
for the chime's sake, since they were reformed
to the tune of a Psalm. She overflows so with the
Bible that she spills it upon every occasion, and will
not cudgel her maids without scripture. It is a
question whether she is more troubled with the
Devil or the Devil with her. She is always challeng-

ing and daring him, and her weapon is *The Practice
of Piety*. Nothing angers her so much as that
women cannot preach, and in this point only thinks
the Brownist erroneous; but what she cannot at
church she does at table, where she prattles more
than any against sense and Antichrist, till a capon's
wing silence her. She expounds the Priests of Baal
"Reading Ministers," and thinks the salvation of
that parish as desperate as the Turks'. She is a
main derider to her capacity of those that are not
her preachers, and censures all sermons but bad
ones. If her husband be a tradesman, she helps
him to customers, howsoever to good cheer, and they
are a most faithful couple at these meetings, for they
never fail. Her conscience is like others' lust, never
satisfied, and you might better answer Scotus' than
her scruples. She is one that thinks she performs
all her duty to God in hearing, and shows the fruits
of it in talking. She is more fiery against the Maypole than her husband, and thinks he might do a
Phineas's act to break the pate of the fiddler. She
is an everlasting argument; but I am weary of her.

53. A SCEPTIC IN RELIGION

Is one that hangs in the balance with all sorts of
opinions, whereof not one but stirs him and none
sways him. A man guiltier of credulity than he is
taken to be; for it is out of his belief of everything
that he fully believes nothing. Each Religion scares
him from its contrary: none persuades him to itself.
He would be wholly a Christian but that he is

something of an Atheist, and wholly an Atheist but
that he is partly a Christian; and a perfect Heretic
but that there are so many to distract him. He
finds reason in all opinions, truth in none: indeed
the least reason perplexes him, and the best will not
satisfy him. He is at most a confused and wild
Christian, not specialised by any form, but capable
of all. He uses the land's Religion because it is
next him, yet he sees not why he may not take the
other, but he chooses this, not as better but because
there is not a pin to choose. He finds doubts and
scruples better than resolves them, and is always
too hard for himself. His learning is too much for
his brain and his judgement too little for his learning,
and his over-opinion of both spoils all. Pity it was
his mischance of being a scholar: for it does only
distract and irregulate him and the world by him.
He hammers much in general upon our opinion's
uncertainty, and the possibility of erring makes him
not venture on what is true. He is troubled at this
naturalness of religion to countries, that Protestantism should be born so in England and Popery
abroad, and that fortune and the stars should so
much share in it. He likes not this connexion of
the Commonweal and Divinity, and fears it may be
an arch-practice of State. In our differences with
Rome he is strangely unfixed, and a new man every
new day, as his last discourse-book's meditations
transport him. He could like the gray hairs of
Popery did not some dotages there stagger him; he
would come to us sooner but our new name affrights
him. He is taken with their miracles but doubts an
imposture; he conceives of our doctrine better, but
it seems too empty and naked. He cannot drive into
his fancy the circumscription of Truth to our
corner, and is as hardly persuaded to think their old
legends true. He approves well of our Faith, and

more of their Works, and is sometimes much affected at the zeal of Amsterdam. His conscience interposes itself betwixt duellers, and whilst it would part both, is by both wounded. He will sometimes propend much to us upon the reading a good writer, and at Bellarmine recoils as far back again; and the Fathers jostle him from one side to another. Now Socinus and Vorstius afresh torture him, and he agrees with none worse than himself. He puts his foot into heresies tenderly, as a cat in the water, and pulls it out again, and still something unanswered delays him, yet he bears away some parcel of each, and you may sooner pick all Religions out of him than one. He cannot think so many wise men should be in error, nor so many honest men out of the way, and his wonder is double when he sees these oppose one another. He hates authority as the tyrant of reason, and you cannot anger him worse than with a Father's *dixit*, and yet that many are not persuaded with reason shall authorise his doubt. In sum, his whole life is a question, and his salvation a greater, which death only concludes, and then he is resolved.

54. AN ATTORNEY

His ancient beginning was a blue coat, since a livery, and his hatching under a Lawyer; whence though but pen-feathered, he hath now nested for himself, and with his hoarded pence purchased an office. Two desks and a quire of paper set him up, where he now sits in state for all comers. We can call him no great author, yet he writes very much, and with the infamy of the court is maintained in his libels. He has some smatch of a scholar, and yet uses Latin very hardly; and lest it should accuse him, cuts it off in the midst, and will not let it speak out. He is contrary to great men, maintained by his followers, that is, his poor country clients, that worship him more than their landlord, and be they never such churls he looks for their courtesy. He first racks them soundly himself, and then delivers them to the Lawyer for execution. His looks are very solicitous, importing much haste and dispatch, he is never without his hands full of business, that is, of paper. His skin becomes at last as dry as his parchment and his face as intricate as the most winding cause. He talks statutes as fiercely as if he had mooted seven years in the Inns of Court; when all his skill is stuck in his girdle, or in his office window. Strife and wrangling have made him rich, and he is thankful to his benefactor, and nourishes it. If he live in a country village, he makes all his neighbours good subjects; for there shall be nothing done but what there is law for. His business gives him not leave to think of his conscience, and when the time, or term, of his life is going out, for Doomsday he is secure; for he hopes he has a trick to reverse judgement.

55. A COWARD

Is the man that is commonly most fierce against the coward, and labouring to take off this suspicion from himself; for the opinion of valour is a good protection to those that dare not use it. No man is valianter than he in civil company and where he thinks no danger may come on it, and is the readiest man to fall upon a drawer and those that must not strike again: wonderful exceptious and choleric where he sees men are loath to give him occasion, and you cannot pacify him better than by quarrelling with him. The hotter you grow, the more temperate man is he; he protests he always honoured you, and the more you rail upon him, the more he honours you, and you threaten him at last into a very honest quiet man. The sight of a sword wounds him more sensibly than the stroke, for before that come he is dead already. Every man is his master that dare beat him, and every man dares that knows him. And he that dare do this is the only man can do much with him; for his friend he cares not for, as a man that carries no such terror as his enemy, which for this cause only is more potent with him of the two. And men fall out with him of purpose to get courtesies from him, and be bribed again to a reconcilement. A man in whom no secret can be bound up, for the apprehension of each danger loosens him, and makes him bewray both the room and it. He is a Christian merely for fear of hell-fire; and if any religion could fright him more, would be of that.

56. A PARTIAL MAN

Is the opposite extreme to a Defamer, for the one speaks ill falsely and the other well, and both slander the truth. He is one that is still weighing men in the scale of comparisons, and puts his affection in the one balance and that sways. His friend always shall do best, and you shall rarely hear good of his enemy. He considers first the man and then the thing, and restrains all merit to what they deserve of him. Commendations he esteems not the debt of worth but the requital of kindness: and if you ask his reason, shews his interest and tells you how much he is beholding to that man. He is one that ties his judgement to the wheel of fortune, and they determine giddily both alike. He prefers England before other countries because he was born there, and Oxford before other Universities because he was brought up there, and the best scholar there is one of his own college, and the best scholar there one of his friends. He is a great favourer of great persons, and his argument is still that which should be antecedent; as, " He is in high place, therefore virtuous "; " he is preferred, therefore worthy." Never ask his opinion, for you shall hear but his faction, and he is indifferent in nothing but conscience. Men esteem him for this a zealous affectionate, but they mistake him many times, for he does it but to be esteemed so. Of all men he is worst to write an History, for he will praise a Sejanus or Tiberius, and for some petty respect of his all posterity shall be cozened.

57. A TRUMPETER

Is the Elephant with the great Trunk, for he eats nothing but what comes through this way. His profession is not so worthy as to occasion insolence, and yet no man so much puffed up. His face is as brazen as his trumpet, and (which is worse) as a fiddler's, from whom he differeth only in this, that his impudence is dearer. The sea of drink and much wind make a storm perpetually in his cheeks, and his look is like his noise, blustering and tempestuous. He was whilom the sound of war, but now of peace; yet as terrible as ever, for wheresoever he comes they are sure to pay for it. He is the common attendant of glittering folks, whether in the court or stage, where he is always the Prologue's Prologue. He is somewhat in the nature of a hogshead, shrillest when he is empty; when his belly is full he is quiet enough. No man proves life more to be a blast, or himself a bubble, and he is like a counterfeit bankrupt, thrives best when he is blown up.

58. A VULGAR-SPIRITED MAN

Is one of the herd of the world. One that follows merely the common cry, and makes it louder by one. A man that loves none but who are publicly affected, and he will not be wiser than the rest of the town. That never owns a friend after an ill name, or some general imputation, though he knows it most unworthy. That opposes to reason, "thus men say," and "thus most do," and "thus the world goes," and thinks this enough to poise the other. That worships men in place, and those only, and thinks all a great man speaks oracles. Much taken with my Lord's jest, and repeats you it all to a syllable. One that justifies nothing out of fashion, nor any opinion out of the applauded way. That thinks certainly all Spaniards and Jesuits very villainous, and is still cursing the Pope and Spinola. One that thinks the gravest cassock the best scholar and the best clothes the finest man. That is taken only with broad and obscene wit, and hisses anything too deep for him. That cries, " Chaucer for his money above all our English poets," because the voice has gone so, and he had read none. That is much ravished with such a nobleman's courtesy, and would venture his life for him because he put off his hat. One that is foremost still to kiss the King's hand, and cries " God bless his Majesty " loudest. That rails on all men condemned and out of favour, and the first that says " away with the Traitors ": yet struck with much ruth at executions, and for pity to see a man die could kill the hangman. That comes to London to see it, and the pretty things in it, and the chief cause of his journey the bears. That measures the happiness of the kingdom by the cheapness of corn; and conceives no harm of state but ill trading. Within this compass too, come those that are too much wedged into the world, and have no lifting thoughts above those things; that call to thrive to do well, and preferment only the grace of God. That aim all studies at this mark, and show you poor scholars as an example to take heed by. That think the prison and want a judgement for some sin, and never like well hereafter of a jail-bird. That know no other content but wealth, bravery, and the town-pleasures; that think all else but idle speculation, and the philosophers madmen. In short, men that are carried away with all outwardnesses, shows, appearances, the stream, the people; for there is no man of worth but has a piece of singularity, and scorns something.

59. A PLODDING STUDENT

Is a kind of Alchemist or persecutor of nature, that would change the dull lead of his brain into finer metal, with success many times as unprosperous, or at least not quitting the cost, to wit, of his own oil and candles. He has a strange forced appetite to learning, and to achieve it brings nothing but patience and a body. His study is not great but continual, and consists much in the sitting up till after midnight in a rug gown and a night-cap, to the vanquishing perhaps of some six lines; yet what he has, he has perfect, for he reads it so long to understand it, till he gets it without book. He may with much industry make a breach into Logic, and arrive at some ability in an argument; but for politer studies he dare not skirmish with them, and for Poetry accounts it impregnable. His invention is no more than the finding out of his papers, and his few gleanings there; and his disposition of them is as just as the book-binder's, a setting or gluing of them together. He is a great discomforter of young students, by telling them what travail it has cost him, and how often his brain turned at philosophy, and makes others fear studying as a cause of duncery. He is a man much given to apothegms which serve him for wit, and seldom breaks any jest but which belonged to some Lacedaimonian or Roman in Lycosthenes. He is like a dull carrier's horse, that will go a whole week together, but never out of a foot-pace; and he that sets forth on the Saturday shall overtake him.

60. A SORDID RICH MAN

Is a beggar of a fair estate, of whose wealth we may say as of other men's unthriftiness, that it has brought him to this: when he had nothing he lived in another kind of fashion. He is a man whom men hate in his own behalf for using himself thus, and yet being upon himself, it is but justice; for he deserves it. Every accession of a fresh heap bates him so much of his allowance, and brings him a degree nearer starving. His body had been long since desperate, but for the reparation of other men's tables, where he hoards meat in his belly for a month, to maintain him in hunger so long. His clothes were never young in our memory; you might make long Epochas from them, and put them into the Almanack with the Dear Year and the Great Frost, and he is known by them longer than his face. He is one never gave alms in his life, and yet is as charitable to his neighbour as himself. He will redeem a penny with his reputation, and lose all his friends to boot; and his reason is he will not be undone. He never pays anything but with strictness of law, for fear of which only he steals not. He

loves to pay short a shilling or two in a great sum,
and is glad to gain that when he can no more. He
never sees friend but in a journey, to save the charges
of an inn, and then only is not sick; and his friends
never see him but to abuse him. He is a fellow
indeed of frantic thrift, and one of the strangest
things that wealth can work.

61. PAUL'S WALK

Is the Land's Epitome, or you may call it the
lesser Isle of Great Britain. It is more than this,
the whole world's map, which you may here discern
in its perfectest motion, jostling and turning. It is
a heap of stones and men, with a vast confusion of
languages; and were the steeple not sanctified,
nothing liker Babel. The noise in it is like that of
bees, a strange humming or buzz, mixed of walking,
tongues and feet: it is a kind of still roar or loud
whisper. It is the great Exchange of all discourse,
and no business whatsoever but is here stirring and
afoot. It is the Synod of all pates politic, jointed
and laid together in most serious posture, and they
are not half so busy at the Parliament. It is the
antic of tails to tails, and backs to backs, and for
vizards you need go no further than faces. It is the
market of young lecturers, whom you may cheapen
here at all rates and sizes. It is the general Mint
of all famous lies, which are here like the legends
of Popery, first coined and stamped in the Church.

All inventions are emptied here, and not few pockets. The best sign of a Temple in it is that is the thieves' sanctuary, which rob more safely in the crowd than a wilderness, whilst every searcher is a bush to hide them. It is the other expense of the day, after plays, tavern, and a bawdy-house; and men have still some oaths left to swear here. It is the ear's brothel, and satisfies their lust and itch. The visitants are all men without exception, but the principal inhabitants and possessors are stale Knights and Captains out of service; men of long rapiers and breeches, which after all turn Merchants here, and traffic for news. Some make it a preface to their dinner, and travel for a stomach: but thriftier men make it their ordinary, and board here very cheap. Of all such places it is least haunted with Hobgoblins, for if a Ghost would walk more he could not.

62. A MERE GREAT MAN

Is so much Heraldry without Honour: himself less real than his title. His virtue is that he was his father's son, and all the expectation of him to beget another. A man that lives merely to preserve another's memory, and let us know who died so many years ago. One of just as much use as his images; only he differs in this that he can speak himself, and save the fellow of Westminster a labour: and he remembers nothing better than what was out of his life. His Grandfathers and their acts are his discourse, and he tells them with more glory than they did them, and it is well that they did enough, or else he had wanted matter. His other studies are his sports, and those vices that are fit for Great Men. Every vanity of his has his officer, and is a serious employment for his servants. He talks loud and bawdily and scurvily as a part of state, and they hear him with reverence. All good qualities are below him, and especially learning, except some parcels of the Chronicle and the writing of his name, which he learns to write, not to be read. He is merely of his servants' faction, and their instrument for their friends and enemies, and is always least thanked for his own courtesies. They that fool him most do most with him, and he little thinks how many laugh at him bare-head. No man is kept in ignorance more of himself and men, for he hears nought but flattery and what is fit to be spoken; truth with so much preface that it loses itself. Thus he lives till his tomb be made ready, and is then a grave statue to prosperity.

63. A COOK

The Kitchen is his Hell, and he the Devil in it, where his meat and he fry together. His revenues are showered down from the fat of the land, and he interlards his own grease among to help the drippings. Choleric he is, not by nature so much as his art, and it is a shrewd temptation that the chopping knife is so near. His weapons ofter offensive are a mess of hot broth and scalding water, and woe be to him that comes in his way. In the kitchen he will domineer and rule the roast in spite of his master, and curses is the very dialect of his calling. His labour is mere blustering and fury, and his speech like that of sailors in a storm, a thousand businesses at once; yet in all this tumult he does not love combustion, but will be the first man that shall go and quench it. He is never a good Christian till a hissing pot of ale has slaked him, like water cast on a firebrand, and for that time he is tame and dispossessed. His cunning is not small in architecture, for he builds strange fabrics in paste, towers and castles, which are offered to the assault of valiant teeth, and like Darius's palace in one banquet demolished. He is a pitiless murderer of Innocents, and he mangles poor fowls with unheard-of tortures, and it is thought the Martyrs' persecutions were devised from hence; sure we are, Saint Lawrence's gridiron came out of his kitchen. His best faculty is at the dresser, where he seems to have great skill in the tactics, ranging his dishes in order military, and placing with great discretion in the forefront meats more strong and hardy and the more cold and cowardly in the rear, as quaking tarts, and quivering custards, and such milk-sop dishes which 'scape many times the fury of the encounter. But now the second course is gone up, and he down into the cellar, where he drinks and sleeps till four o'clock in the afternoon, and then returns again to his regiment.

64. A BOLD FORWARD MAN

Is a lusty fellow in a crowd, that's beholden more
to his elbow than his legs, for he does not go but
thrusts well. He is a good shuffler in the world,
wherein he is so oft putting forth, that at length he
puts on. He can do some things, but dare do much
more, and is like a desperate soldier, who will assault
anything where he is sure not to enter. He is not
so well opinioned of himself as industrious to make
other; and thinks no vice so prejudicial as blushing.
He is still citing for himself that a candle should
not be hid under a bushel, and for his part, he will
be sure not to hide his, though his candle be but a
snuff or rush-candle. These few good parts he has,
he is no niggard in displaying, and is like some needy
flaunting goldsmith, nothing in the inner room but
all on the cupboard. If he be a scholar, he has
commonly stepped into the pulpit before a degree;
yet into that too before he deserved it. He never
defers St. Mary's beyond his regency, and his next
Sermon is at Paul's Cross, and that printed. He
loves public things alife: and for any solemn entertainment he will find a mouth, find a speech who
will. He is greedy of great acquaintance and many,
and thinks it no small advancement to rise to be
known. He is one that has all the great names at
Court at his fingers' ends, and their lodgings, and with
a saucy " My Lord " will salute the best of them.
His talk at the table is like Benjamin's mess, five
times to his part, and no argument shuts him out
for a quarreller. Of all disgraces he endures not to
be nonplussed, and had rather fly for sanctuary to
nonsense, which few can descry, than to nothing,
which all. His boldness is beholden to other men's
modesty, which rescues him many times from a

baffle; yet his face is good armour, and he is dashed out of anything sooner than countenance. Grosser conceits are puzzled in him for a rare man; and wiser men, though they know him, yet take him in for their pleasure, or as they would do a sculler for being next at hand. Thus preferment at last stumbles on him because he is still in the way. His companions that flouted him before now envy him, when they see him come ready for scarlet, whilst themselves lie musty in their old clothes and colleges.

65. A BAKER

No man verifies the proverb more, that it is an alms-deed to punish him; for his penalty is a dole and does the beggars as much good as their dinner. He abhors therefore works of charity, and thinks his bread cast away when it is given to the poor. He loves not Justice neither, for the weigh-scales' sake, and hates the Clerk of the Market as his executioner; yet he finds mercy in his offences, and his basket only is sent to prison. Marry, a pillory is his deadly enemy, and he never hears well after.

66. A PRETENDER TO LEARNING

Is one that would make all others more fools than himself; for though he know nothing, he would not have the world know so much. He conceits nothing in learning but the opinion, which he seeks to purchase without it, though he might with less labour cure his ignorance than hide it. He is indeed a kind of Scholar-Mountebank, and his art our delusion. He is tricked out in all the accoutrements of learning, and at the first encounter none passes better. He is oftener in his study than at his book, and you cannot pleasure him better than to deprehend him: yet he hears you not till the third knock, and then comes out very angry, as interrupted. You will find him in his slippers, and a pen in his ear, in which formality he was asleep. His table is spread wide with some Classic Folio, which is as constant to it as the carpet, and hath laid open in the same page this half year. His candle is always a longer sitter-up than himself, and the boast of his window at midnight. He walks much alone in the posture of meditation, and has a book still before his face in the fields. His pocket is seldom without a Greek Testament, or Hebrew Bible, which he opens only in Church, and that when some stander-by looks over. He has his sentences for company, some scatterings of Seneca and Tacitus, which are good upon all occasions. If he reads anything in the morning, it comes up all at dinner; and as long as that lasts, the discourse is his. He is a great plagiary of tavern-wit, and comes to sermons only that he may talk of Austin. His parcels are the mere scrapings from company, yet he complains at parting what time he has lost. He is wondrously capricious to seem a judgement, and listens with a sour attention to what he understands not. He talks much of Scaliger and Casaubon and the Jesuits, and prefers some unheard-of Dutch name before them all. He has verses to bring in upon these and these hints, and it shall go hard but he will wind in his opportunity. He is critical in a language he cannot construe, and speaks seldom under Arminius in divinity. His business and retirement and caller away is his study, and he protests no delight to it comparable. He is a great nomenclator of authors, which he has read in general in the catalogue, and in particular in the title, and goes seldom so far as the Dedication. He never talks of anything but learning, and learns all from talking. Three encounters with the same men pump him, and then he only puts in or gravely says nothing. He has taken pains to be an ass, though not to be a scholar, and is at length discovered and laughed at.

67. A POOR MAN

Is the most impotent man, though neither blind nor lame, as wanting the more necessary limbs of life, without which limbs are a burden. A man unfenced and unsheltered from the gusts of the world, which blow all in upon him, like an unroofed house; and the bitterest thing he suffers is his neighbours. All men put on to him a kind of churlisher fashion, and even more plausible natures churlish to him, as who are nothing advantaged by his opinion. Whom men fall out with before-hand to prevent friendship, and his friends too to prevent engagements, or if they own him 'tis in private and a by-room, and on condition not to know them before company. All vice put together is not half so scandalous, nor sets off our acquaintance further, and even those that are not friends for ends do not love any dearness with such men. The least courtesies are upbraided to him, and himself thanked for none; but his best services suspected as hand-some sharking and tricks to get money. And we shall observe it in knaves themselves, that your beggarliest knaves are the greatest, or thought so at least, for those that have wit to thrive by it have art not to seem so. Now a poor man has not vizard enough to mask his vices, nor ornament enough to set forth his virtues; but both are naked and unhandsome: and though no man is necessitated to more ill, yet no man's ill is less excused, but it is thought a kind of impudence in him to be vicious, and a presumption above his fortune. His good parts lie dead upon his hands for want of matter to employ them, and at the best are not commended but pitied, as virtues ill placed; and we say of him, " 'Tis an honest man, but 'tis pity ": and yet those that call him so will trust a knave before him. He is a man that has the truest speculation of the world, because all men show to him in their plainest and worst, as a man they have no plot on by appearing good to; whereas rich men are entertained with a more holiday behaviour, and see only the best we can dissemble. He is the only he that tries the true strength of wisdom, what it can do of itself without the help of fortune; that with a great deal of virtue conquers extremities, and with a great deal more his own impatience, and obtains of himself not to hate men.

68. A HERALD

Is the spawn, or indeed but the resultancy of Nobility, and to the making of him went not a generation, but a genealogy. His trade is honour, and he sells it, and gives arms himself, though he be no gentleman. His bribes are like those of a corrupt judge; for they are the prices of blood. He seems very rich in discourse, for he tells you of whole fields of gold and silver, Or and Argent, worth much in French, but in English nothing. He is a great diver in the streams or issues of Gentry, and not a by-channel or bastard escapes him; yea he does with them like some shameless quean, fathers more children than ever they begot. His traffic is a kind of pedlary-ware, scutchions and pennons and little daggers and lions, such as children esteem and gentlemen: but his pennyworths are rampant, for you may buy three whole brawns cheaper than three boars' heads of him painted. He was sometimes the terrible Coat of Mars, but is now for more merciful battles in the Tilt-yard, where whosoever is victorious, the spoils are his. He is an art in England, but in Wales nature, where they are born with Heraldry in their mouths, and each name is a pedigree.

69. THE COMMON SINGING-MEN IN CATHEDRAL CHURCHES

Are a bad society, and yet a company of good fellows, that roar deep in the choir, deeper in the tavern. They are the eight parts of speech, which go to the Syntaxis of Service, and are distinguished by their noises much like bells, for they make not a consort but a peal. Their pastime or recreation is prayers, their exercise drinking, yet herein so religiously addicted that they serve God oftest when they are drunk. Their humanity is a leg to the Residencer, their learning a chapter, for they learn it commonly before they read it; yet the old Hebrew names are little beholden to them, for they miscall them worse than one another. Though they never expound the scripture they handle it much, and pollute the Gospel with two things, their conversation and their thumbs. Upon worky-days they behave themselves at prayers as at their pots, for they swallow them down in an instant. Their gowns are laced commonly with streamings of ale, the superfluities of a cup or throat above measure. Their skill in melody makes them the better companions abroad, and their anthems abler to sing catches. Long-lived for the most part they are not, especially the base, they overflow their bank so oft to drown the organs. Briefly, if they escape arresting, they die constantly in God's service; and to take their death with more patience, they have wine and cakes at their funeral: and now they keep the Church a great deal better, and help to fill it with their bones as before with their noise.

70. A SHOPKEEPER

His Shop is his well-stuffed book, and himself the title-page of it, or index. He utters much to all men, though he sells but to a few, and intreats for his own necessities by asking others what they lack. No man speaks more and no more, for his words are like his wares, twenty of one sort, and he goes over them alike to all comers. He is an arrogant commender of his own things; for whatsoever he shews you is the best in the town, though the worst in his shop. His conscience was a thing that would have laid upon his hands, and he was forced to put it off, and makes great use of honesty to profess upon. He tells you lies by rote, and not minding, as the phrase to sell in, and the language he spent most of his years to learn. He never speaks so truly as when he says he would use you as his brother, for he would abuse his brother; and in his shop thinks it lawful. His Religion is much in the nature of his customers, and indeed the pander to it: and by a misinterpreted sense of Scripture " makes a gain of his Godliness." He is your slave while you pay him ready money, but if he once befriend you your tyrant, and you had better deserve his hate than his trust.

71. A BLUNT MAN

Is one whose wit is better pointed than his behaviour, and that coarse and unpolished, not out of ignorance so much as humour. He is a great enemy to the fine gentleman, and these things of compliment, and hates ceremony in conversation as the Puritan in religion. He distinguishes not betwixt fair and double dealing, and suspects all smoothness for the dress of knavery. He starts at the encounter of a salutation as an assault, and beseeches you in choler to forbear your courtesy. He loves not anything in discourse that comes before the purpose, and is always suspicious of a preface. Himself falls rudely still on his matter without any circumstance, except he use an old proverb for an introduction. He swears old out-of-date innocent oaths, as " by the Mass," " by our Lady," and such like, and though there be Lords present, he cries, " My Masters." He is exceedingly in love with his humour, which makes him always profess and proclaim it, and you must take what he says patiently, " because he is a plain man." His nature is his excuse still, and other men's tyrant; for he must speak his mind, and that is his worst, and craves your pardon most injuriously for not pardoning you. His jests best become him, because they come from him rudely and unaffected; and he has the luck commonly to have them famous. He is one that will do more than he will speak, and yet speak more than he will hear; for though he love to touch others, he is touchy himself, and seldom to his own abuses replies but with his fists. He is as squeazy of his commendations as his courtesy, and his good word is like an eulogy in a satire. He is generally better favoured than he favours, as being commonly well expounded in his bitterness, and no man speaks treason more securely. He chides great men with most boldness, and is counted for it an honest fellow. He is grumbling much in the behalf of the commonwealth, and is in prison oft for it with credit. He is generally honest, but more generally thought so, and his downrightness credits him, as a man not well bended and crook-kneed to the times. In conclusion, he is not easily bad in whom this quality is nature, but the counterfeit is most dangerous since he is disguised in a humour that professes not to disguise.

72. A HANDSOME HOSTESS

Is the fairer commendation of an Inn, above the fair sign or fair lodgings. She is the loadstone that attracts men of iron, gallants and roarers, where they cleave sometimes long, and are not easily got off. Her lips are your welcome, and your entertainment her company, which is put into the reckoning too, and is the dearest parcel in it. No Citizen's wife is demurer than she at the first greeting, nor draws in her mouth with a chaster simper; but you may be more familiar without distaste, and she does not startle at bawdry. She is the confusion of a pottle of sack more than would have been spent elsewhere, and her little jugs are accepted to have her kiss excuse them. She may be an honest woman but is not believed so in her parish, and no man is a greater infidel in it than her husband.

73. A CRITIC

Is one that has spelled over a great many of books, and his observation is the orthography. He is the surgeon of old authors, and heals the wounds of dust and ignorance. He converses much in fragments and *Desunt multa's* and if he piece it up with two lines he is more proud of that book than the author. He runs over all sciences to peruse their syntaxis, and thinks all learning comprised in writing Latin. He tastes styles as some discreeter palates do wine; and tells you which is genuine, which sophisticate and bastard. His own phrase is a miscellany of old words, deceased long before the Caesars, and entombed by Varro, and the modernest man he follows is Plautus. He writes " Omneis " at length, and " quicquid," and his Gerund is most inconformable. He is a troublesome vexer of the dead, which after so long sparing must rise up to the judgement of his castigations. He is one that makes all books sell dearer, whilst he swells them into folios with his comments.

74. A SERGEANT, OR CATCH-POLE

Is one of God's judgements; and which our roarers do only conceive terrible. He is the properest shape wherein they fancy Satan; for he is at most but an Arrester, and Hell a dungeon. He is the creditors' hawk, wherewith they seize upon flying birds, and fetch them again in his talons. He is the period of young Gentlemen, or their full stop, for when he meets with them they can go no farther. His ambush is a shop-stall, or close lane, and his assault is cowardly at your back. He respites you in no place but a tavern, where he sells his minutes dearer than a clock-maker. The common way to run from him is through him, which is often attempted and achieved, and no man is more beaten out of charity. He is one makes the street more dangerous than the highways, and men go better provided in their walks than their journey. He is the first handsel of the young rapiers of the Templars, and they are as proud of his repulse as an Hungarian of killing a Turk. He is a moveable Prison, and his hands two manacles hard to be filed off. He is an occasioner of disloyal thoughts in the Commonwealth, for he makes men hate the King's name worse than the Devil's.

75. AN ORDINARY HONEST MAN

Is one whom it concerns to be called honest, for if he were not this he were nothing: and yet he is not this neither, but a good dull vicious fellow, that complies well with the deboshments of the time, and is fit for it. One that has no good part in him to offend his company, or make him to be suspected a proud fellow; but is sociably a dunce, and sociably a drinker. That does it fair and above-board without legerdemain, and neither sharks for a cup or a reckoning. That is kind o'er his beer, and protests he loves you, and begins to you again, and loves you again. One that quarrels with no man but for not pledging him, but takes all absurdities and commits as many, and is no tell-tale next morning, though he remember it. One that will fight for his friend if he hear him abused, and his friend commonly is he that is most likely, and he lifts up many a jug in his defence. He rails against none but censurers, against whom he thinks he rails lawfully, and censurers are all those that are better than himself. These good properties qualify him for honesty enough, and raise him high in the Ale-house commendation, who, if he had any other good quality, would be named by that. But now for refuge he is an honest man, and hereafter a sot. Only those that commend him think not so, and those that commend him are honest fellows.

76. AN UNIVERSITY DUN

Is a Gentleman's follower cheaply purchased, for his own money has hired him. He is an inferior creditor of some ten shillings or downwards, contracted for horse-hire or perchance for drink, too weak to be put in suit, and he arrests you modestly. He is now very expensive of his time, for he will wait upon your stairs a whole afternoon, and dance attendance with more patience than a Gentleman-

Usher. He is a sore beleaguerer of chambers, and
assaults them sometimes with furious knocks; yet
finds strong resistance commonly, and is kept out.
He is a great complainer of scholars' loitering, for he
is sure never to find them within, and yet he is the
chief cause many times that makes them study. He
grumbles at the ingratitude of men that shun him
for his kindness, but indeed it is his own fault, for
he is too great an upbraider. No man puts them
more to their brain than he; and by shifting him off
they learn to shift in the world. Some choose their
rooms on purpose to avoid his surprisals, and think
the best commodity in them his prospect. He is like
a rejected acquaintance, hunts those that care not
for his company; and he knows it well enough and
yet will not keep away. The sole place to supple
him is the buttery, where he takes grievous use upon
your name, and he is one much wrought with good
beer and rhetoric. He is a man of most unfortunate
voyages, and no gallant walks the street to less
purpose.

77. A STAID MAN

Is a Man. One that has taken order with himself,
and set a rule to those lawlessnesses within him.
Whose life is distinct and in method, and his actions
as it were cast up before. Not loosed into the
world's vanities, but gathered up and contracted in
his station. Not scattered into many pieces of
businesses, but that one course he takes, goes

through with. A man firm and standing in his purposes, not heaved off with each wind and passion. That squares his expense to his coffers, and makes the total first and then the items. One that thinks what he does, and does what he says, and foresees what he may do before he purposes. One whose " if I can " is more than another's assurance; and his doubtful tale before some men's protestations. That is confident of nothing in futurity, yet his conjectures oft true prophecies. That makes a pause still betwixt his ear and belief, and is not too hasty to say after others. One whose tongue is strung up like a clock till the time, and then strikes, and says much when he talks little. That can see the truth betwixt two wranglers, and sees them agree even in that they fall out upon. That speaks no rebellion in a bravery, or talks big from the spirit of sack. A man cool and temperate in his passions, not easily betrayed by his choler. That vies not oath with oath, nor heat with heat; but replies calmly to an angry man, and is too hard for him too. That can come fairly off from Captains' companies, and neither drink nor quarrel. One whom no ill hunting sends home discontented, and makes him swear at his dogs and family. One not hasty to pursue the new fashion, nor yet affectedly true to his old round breeches; but gravely handsome, and to his place, which suits him better than his tailor. Active in the world without disquiet, and careful without misery; yet neither ingulfed in his pleasures, nor a seeker of business, but has his hours for both. A man that seldom laughs violently, but his mirth is a cheerful look. Of a composed and settled countenance, not set, nor much alterable with sadness or joy. He affects nothing so wholly that he must be a miserable man when he loses it; but forethinks what will come hereafter, and spares Fortune his thanks and curses. One that loves his credit, not this word "Reputation"; yet can save both without a duel: whose entertainments to greater men are respectful not complimentary, and to his friends plain not rude. A good husband, father, master; that is, without doting, pampering, familiarity. A man well poised in all humours; in whom Nature shewed most Geometry, and he has not spoiled the work. A man of more wisdom than wittiness, and brain than fancy; and abler to anything than to make Verses.

78. A SUSPICIOUS OR JEALOUS MAN

Is one that watches himself a mischief, and keeps a leer eye still for fear it should escape him. A man that sees a great deal more in everything than is to be seen, and yet he thinks he sees nothing. His own eye stands in his light. He is a fellow commonly guilty of some weaknesses, which he might conceal if he were careless: now his over-diligence to hide them makes men pry the more. Howsoever he imagines you have found him, and it shall go hard but you must abuse him whether you will or no. Not a word can be spoke but nips him somewhere; not a jest thrown out but he will make it hit him. You shall have him go fretting out of company, with some twenty quarrels to every man, stung and galled, and no man knows less the occasion than they that have given it. To laugh before him is a dangerous matter, for it cannot be at anything but at him, and to whisper in his company plain conspiracy. He bids you speak out and he will answer you, when you thought not of him. He expostulates with you in passion, why you should abuse him, and explains to your ignorance wherein, and gives you very good reason, at last, to laugh at him hereafter. He is one still accusing others when they are not guilty, and defending himself when he is not accused: and no man is undone more with apologies, wherein he is so elaborately excessive that none will believe him; and he is never thought worse of, than when he has given satisfaction. Such men can never have friends, because they cannot trust so far: and this humour hath this infection with it, it makes all men to them suspicious. In conclusion, they are men always in offence and vexation with themselves and their neighbours, wronging others in thinking they would wrong them, and themselves most of all in thinking they deserve it.

NOTES.

1. A CHILD.
Page 9.

This *Character* is one of the most delicately delineated miniatures of childhood in our literature. It expresses without sentimentality the sentimental attitude towards childhood, the attitude which is for most people associated with the saying of Jesus Christ: " Suffer little children to come unto me and forbid them not: for of such is the kingdom of God," and for admirers of the *Golden Treasury* associated with Wordsworth's *Ode on Intimations of Immortality from Recollections of Early Childhood.* A studied comparison of this poem with Earle's *Character* is well repaid. Earle has more of freshness and delicacy than the poet and is not less profound. For while Wordsworth employs the emotive associations of hinted metaphysical doctrines in aid of heightened sentimentalism, both writers are in fact expressing an adult attitude to the fact of childhood and not presenting an objective analysis of the child-mind.

The idea of the pristine purity of the child is peculiarly Christian and, despite the antipathetic doctrine of Original Sin, has been a growing influence on the general attitude of Christian peoples until modern times. Its value is obvious; but, as ever happens when a doctrine is based upon sentiment, it has tended to depreciate understanding. Now that its influence is balanced by a more scientific attitude, we may hope that what it has of value will be maintained, while its sentimentalities will be tempered by saner understanding.

The philosophical analogue of Earle's attitude found expression some years later in Locke's doctrine of the *tabula rasa,* the doctrine, namely, that the mind is at birth a " blank slate " upon which are written by life and experience all the characteristics and dispositions of the adult.

CHARACTER: contains the three meanings *letter* (referring to line 1), *moral character,* and *character sketch* such as Earle himself is writing. This pregnant use of words is a characteristic of the " wit " which belongs to the seventeenth century in general and to Charactery in particular.

OIL: the invention of oil painting is usually attributed to John van Eyck (1385-1441), the founder of the Flemish school. Painting in England was killed during the Hundred Years' War and there was no national art until the eighteenth century. But a few foreign masters were welcomed and Holbein, Anthony Mor, Rubens, and Van Dyck almost became English painters.

WHITE PAPER . . . NOTE-BOOK: an interesting anticipation of Locke. The doctrines of the philosophers are often "in the air" and are crystallised and formalised into a system only by them.

PURELY HAPPY: completely happy; possessed of happiness *unalloyed*. (With a characteristic play on the other sense of the word.)

TICE: entice.

LIKE HIS FIRST FATHER . . . BREECHES: like Adam, the child has lost his pristine innocence when he attains to breeches. "As a child advances in age, he commonly proceeds in the knowledge and commission of vice and immorality." (Bliss.) Emphasis is upon the purity of the child rather than the wickedness of the man. The reference is to Genesis, iii. 7. In the English translation of the Bible issued at Geneva in 1559 the word "breeches" is used in this verse where the Authorised Version of 1611 has "aprons."
The doctrines of the Fall and of Original Sin were very much to the fore at this time, being strenuously insisted upon by the Puritans.

OLD MAN'S RELAPSE: the sentiment that old age is a second childhood is a commonplace of the Character writers. In his *Character of an Old Man*, Wye Saltonstall says: "Though the proverb be 'Once a man and twice a child,' yet he hopes from his second childhood to run back into his teens and so be twice a man too."

LITTLE COAT: *i.e.* petticoat. The child "puts off his petticoat" when he is breeched.

2. A YOUNG RAW PREACHER.
Page 10.

TRUANTED: scamped the full course of training. The full course is given by contrast in the next *Character*.

HASTY: contains the two meanings "had not been a divine so soon" and "rash" or "precipitate."

TABLE-BOOK: tablets or note-book. The modern equivalent is " lecture-notes."

COLLECTIONS OF STUDY: notes from his studies.

ST. MARY'S: at Oxford, where the University Sermons are still preached. Earle hints at the impropriety of hashed-up University Sermons for country congregations.

BRACHIGRAPHY: Bliss is followed by West in assigning the introduction of *shorthand* into this country to Peter Bales, who published in 1590 *The Writing Schoolmaster*, the first part of which dealt with " Brachygraphie, that is, to write as fast as a man speaketh treatably, writing but one letter for a word." But Timothy Bright introduced his system two years earlier than that, in his *Characterie: an Arte of Shorte, Swifte, and Secrete Writing by Character*.

Throughout the Middle Ages the system invented by Tiro, the freedman of Cicero, was widely used. The introduction of systems based on the alphabet began with the publication in 1602 of the *Arte of Stenographie* by John Willis. Through the seventeenth century there was considerable interest in systems of shorthand writing. Samuel Pepys used the system of Thomas Shelton (published about 1630) in keeping his Diary.

GETS WITHOUT BOOK: learns off by heart. But here there is a play upon the *literal* meaning, *i.e.* hears in other people's sermons.

ACCOMPLISHED: equipped.

CONCEITED: full of conceits, or pedantic mannerisms; fantastic.

REMEMBERS HIS COLLEGE MORE AT LARGE: this refers to the commemoration of the founders and benefactors of the preacher's own college, in the prayer appointed to precede the University Sermon. This becomes a mere impertinence before a country congregation. " at large " probably means " lengthily," or perhaps " without discrimination."

CLOCK: Hook says (*Church Dict.*): " For the measurement of the time of a sermon hour-glasses were frequently attached to pulpits." The hour-glass or pulpit clock was a larger version of the egg-timer still occasionally used. *Cf.* Fuller: " America is not unfitly resembled to an Houre-glasse, which hath a narrow neck of land . . . betwixt the parts thereof." The normal time of a sermon was the hour. Only exceptional preachers would turn over the clock and proceed into the second hour.

IN LAVENDER: stored up among his University gleanings.

BELLARMINE: "Robert Bellarmin, an Italian jesuit, was born at Monte Pulciano, a town in Tuscany, in the year 1542, and in 1560 entered himself among the jesuits.   In 1599 he was honoured with a cardinal's hat, and in 1602 was presented with the archbishopric of Capua: this, however, he resigned in 1605, when Pope Paul V. desired to have him near himself. He was employed in the affairs of the court of Rome till 1621, when, leaving the Vatican, he retired to a house belonging to his order, and died September 17, in the same year.

"Bellarmin was one of the best controversial writers of his time; few authors have done greater honour to their profession or opinions, and certain it is that none have ever more ably defended the cause of the Romish Church, or contended in favour of the pope with greater advantage. As a proof of Bellarmin's abilities, there was scarcely a divine of any eminence among the protestants who did not attack him: Bayle aptly says, ' they made his name resound everywhere, *ut littus Styla, Styla, omne sonaret.*' "—(Bliss.)

His name was the more in men's minds in England because of the controversy with King James I., begun by James' *Apologia pro Juramento Fidelitatis* (1609, published anonymously in 1607) and continued by Andrewes on the King's behalf.

ACTION . . . PASSION: the verbal antithesis is a characteristic of this *genre* of writing.   The special meaning of "action" here is, of course, "oratorical gesture."

SEVERAL: different.

EXTRAORDINARY: (adverb) chiefly.

HANDKERCHER: spelt according to the general pronunciation at the time. Mr. A. S. West quotes from Thackeray's description of the Rev. Charles Honeyman in *The Newcomes* (Ch. VIII.): "No man in London understood the pocket-handkerchief business better, or smothered his emotion more beautifully."

NEVER LOOKS UPON BOOK: preaches without notes.

POSTILS: commentaries.   The word is from the Medieval Latin *postilla* (*post illa*), deriving from marginal annotations which follow the text.

TOWN-PRECISIAN : "precisian" was a common, and slightly derogatory, appellation of the Puritans, deriving from their "preciseness" or scrupulosity in religious ceremonial.

FRIDAY NIGHTS: Earle implies that the Puritan, in his eagerness to be at variance with the Church ceremonial, makes a habit of feasting on Friday, the orthodox fast day. Compare Overbury: "If at any time he fast it is upon Sunday, and he is sure to feast upon Friday." (Character of *A Precisian*). The Puritans objected to the Church Festivals as having no authority in scripture or primitive Christianity.

YOU SHALL KNOW . . .: in an age when extravagant and tasteless display was the rule as costume grew ever more elaborate, the Puritans affected a plainness and simplicity of which they were no less fanatically vain than the gallants were vain of their costly and ridiculous finery. The following song, revived in the Civil War period from a play of 1602, gives an amusing picture of either affectation:—

> She told me that I was too much profane,
>   And not devout, neither in speech nor gesture;
> And I could not one word answer again,
>   Nor had not so much grace to call her sister;
> For ever something did offend her there,
> Either my broad beard, hat, or my long hair.
>
> My band was broad, my 'parel was not plain,
>   My points and girdle made the greatest show;
> My sword was odious, and my belt was vain,
>   My Spanish shoes were cut too broad at toe !
> My stockings light, my garters tied too long,
> My gloves perfumed, and had a scent too strong.
>
> I left my pure mistress for a space,
>   And to a snip-snap barber straight went I;
> I cut my hair, and did my corps uncase
>   Of 'parel's pride that did offend the eye;
> My high-crowned hat, my little beard also
> My pecked band, my shoes were sharp at toe.
>
> Gone was my sword, and my belt was laid aside,
>   And I transformed both in looks and speech;
> My 'parel plain, my cloak was void of pride,
>   My little skirts, my metamorphos'd breech,
> My stockings black, my garters were tied shorter,
> My gloves no scent; thus marched I to her porter.

The short hair of the Puritans was the origin of the term "Roundheads." The gallants, on the other hand, allowed their hair to grow long and matted. The *cape* is the upper part of the cloak turned down over the shoulders. These had become very gorgeous. The *ruff* is the large circular collar familiar from pictures of the Elizabethans. They were often worn of ridiculous size, stiffened with coloured starch and elaborately pleated.

CHAMBERMAID: West quotes Macaulay (*History of England*, Vol. I., pp. 325-9) on the social position of the English clergy after the Reformation: " It would not be easy to find, in the comedy of the seventeenth century, a single instance of a clergyman who wins a spouse above the rank of a cook."

THIRTY POUNDS: the writers of *Shakespeare's England* estimated in 1916 that Elizabethan money must be multiplied by five or six to represent its modern value. Thirty pounds a year at that time represented a small, but by no means exceptionally small, stipend for a clergyman.

3. A GRAVE DIVINE.

Page 12.

Bliss aptly quotes Chaucer's " poure Persone " with this Character. These two are, indeed, the finest miniatures in our language of the parson at his best. Nor, if this was his youthful ideal, did Earle fall far short of it himself. Thus speaks Walton of him in the *Life of Mr. Richard Hooker:* " Dr. Earle, now Lord Bishop of Salisbury, of whom I may justly say . . . that, since Mr. Hooker died, none have lived whom God hath blessed with more innocent wisdom, more sanctified learning, or a more pious, peaceable, primitive temper: so that this excellent person seems to be only like himself, and our venerable Richard Hooker."

Normally the B.A. was taken at the end of nine terms, and represented a fairly wide reading in the classics and training in scholastic philosophy, under the aegis of Aristotle. Theological students who took a full course continued a further three years.

EXPECTED: awaited.

ARTS refers to the Arts degree, and HUMANE READING (*litterae humaniores*) at this time referred almost exclusively to reading of the classics. We still use the term " humanities " in this connotation.

SCHOOL-DIVINITY: theology of the schools or universities. This was still almost completely scholastic in its formal character.

SOUNDED: plumbed.

BOTH RELIGIONS: Roman Catholicism and Protestantism.

ENFORCED ACTION: strained gesticulation.

HE COMES NOT UP . . .: the Puritans advocated frequent and lengthy sermons. Earle is here obliquely poking fun at this prepossession. He implies that they, in contrast to his ideal divine, preach *often* for want of anything better to do, and *long* in the vain endeavour to say something more than empty words.

CONVERSATION: daily habit of life.

CEREMONIOUS: fastidious. In the long drawn-out struggle between Puritanism and ecclesiasticism "ceremonies were a convenient battle-ground on which the rival contentions met, the puritan maintaining that no ceremonies might be imposed which were not authorised by the Bible, the churchman insisting that such ceremonies might be imposed by church authority which were not contrariant to the Bible."—(W. H. Frere, *A History of the English Church* 1558-1625). Earle's grave Divine thinks it a more serious matter to be at schism with his church than to conform in such minor matters as the wearing of a surplice. These were burning questions of the day, and upon them every young student of divinity, and Earle himself, must reach a decision which would influence for better or for worse his whole career. The question of vestments and in particular the surplice has always been a most heated article of controversy. There were also serious attacks upon the Episcopal system (*the Church's Hierarchy*), which culminated in the Church of the Commonwealth.

SIMONIACAL PURCHASES: Simony is the buying and selling of ecclesiastical appointments. At the dissolution of the monasteries the larger part of the endowments had gone into lay hands, and these new patrons "made no shame even of open simony." Despite legislation in 1559, Elizabeth herself, and favourites such as Sir Walter Raleigh and Sir Francis Carew, made immense sums from the sale of preferments. "With such an example before them it is not surprising that the nobility and gentry followed suit at a respectful distance in their own sphere. Thus both dioceses and parishes had been simoniacally robbed, partly by direct alienations and partly by fraudulent leases; and both the clergy and the benefices steadily deteriorated."—(Frere.)

GRATER: skinflint.

BY WHOM HE IS SPITED . . . QUARRELS: who is vexed with him for making up quarrels.

4. A MODEST MAN.
Page 13.

PUT . . . INJURY: pocket any insult.

YOUR IRONY: the modest man understands praise as irony.

THREATENS: the word "threaten" is used of *undesirable* things in the sense of *impend, e.g.* "Danger threatens us." By a curious contraction of phrase Earle shows by the use of this word that the Modest Man regards as a *threat* what other men would regard as desirable. There is no parallel for West's rendering "terrifies." "Threatens" is not used in a different *sense*, but in a phrase of unusual compression.

DEPREHENDED: surprised; found out.

HE EXCUSES . . . SATISFIED: he finds excuse for faults in you which others would lay to your charge, and is satisfied if you will pardon him his own faults.

TENDER: sensitive.

5. A MERE DULL PHYSICIAN.
Page 15.

EMPIRIC: this term was commonly employed in the sense of "quack." Literally it means one whose knowledge is based upon trial and error and not upon the theoretical principles of his craft. *Cf.* below, "his skill is merely opinion."

ROUND VELVET CAP: the term "velvet cap" is used of a doctor in *The Return from Parnassus* (1606). Velvet was much worn by the gentry in the sixteenth and seventeenth centuries. In Elizabeth's time the hats of the fashionable were generally of velvet. The *flat cap* was enjoined by Act of Parliament in 1571 (repealed in 1597) on citizens, artificers, and labourers. As late as 1630 Decker wrote, in *The Honest Whore:*

> "Flat caps as proper are to city gowns,
> As to armour helmets, or to kings their crowns."

These caps were, however, of wool. "Thrummed" caps are mentioned in *The Knight of the Burning Pestle* as worn by apprentices, and the common people wore their hats of felt. Thus the *velvet cap* was distinctive at this time. Caps were round and low in the brim; the general form survives in the caps of the Blue-coat boys of Christ's Hospital.

But *caps* also played a part in the elaborate ceremonial of the conferring of the doctorate at the University, and Earle, as he plays upon the double meaning of "doctor," so also certainly refers here to this practice. "In the Elizabethan statutes the Doctors were called emphatically *pileati*, cap-wearers. Bentley explains the solemn delivery of the *Cap* to the Inceptor to mean that he was free, and also that he was to set out on a toilsome journey, eloquent like Ulysses, cunning like Mercury, workman-like as Vulcan: the three who are especially represented in antiques with *petasi*."—(Wordsworth, *University Life in Eighteenth Century*, pp. 255-256.) This oblique reference to the solemn ceremonial of the cap in the doctorate enhances the ludicrousness of Earle's punning comparison of the ignorant medical practitioner with the University Doctor.

GALEN: (about A.D. 130-200). A Greek physician and philosopher. He was the most eminent physician of antiquity after Hippocrates. He wrote 500 treatises, of which 124 were devoted to philosophy. His philosophical importance is in the transmission of the Peripatetic doctrines of his own day. His medical works were widely read in the Middle Ages, and until the era of modern medicine he was regarded as the ultimate authority in medicine.

HYPOCRATES: a Greek physician, about 460 B.C. Little or nothing is known about the life of Hippocrates, although there are masses of legend. He has been universally venerated as the "Father of Medicine." A collection of medical treatises has come down to us under his name, and some of these may be actually from his pen.

APHORISMS: in the "aphoristic" style, which is adopted in several treatises in the Hippocratean *corpus*, important and far-reaching conclusions are compressed into short, easily remembered sentences. The treatise entitled *Aphorisms* opens with the famous sentence, " Art is long and Life is short."

In Scene I. of Marlowe's *Doctor Faustus* Galen is first invoked by Faustus, when he decides to abandon philosophy for medicine. His mastery of that science is expressed in the line,

" Is not thy common talk sound *aphorisms ?* "

Galen and Hippocrates were by the Elizabethan Statutes of 1570 appointed to be the textbooks of the lectures in Medicine at Cambridge.

ALEXIS OF PIEMONT: " *The secretes of the reverende maister Alexis of Piemount, containyng excellente remedies against divers diseases, etc.*, appear to have been a very favourite study either with physicians, or their patients, about this period. . . . A specimen of the importance of this publication may be given in the title of the first secret, ' The maner and secrete to conserve a man's youth, and to holde back olde age, to maintain a man always in helth and strength, as in the fayrest floure of his yeres.' *The Regiment of Helthe*, by Thomas Paynell, is another volume of the same description."—(Bliss.)

SUPERSCRIPTIONS OF GALLYPOTS: " titles on medicine bottles." Gallipots were small glazed jars in which medicine was kept.

VESPATIAN'S RULE: " Vespatian, tenth emperor of Rome, imposed a tax upon urine, and when his son Titus remonstrated with him on the meanness of the act, ' Pecuniam,' says Suetonius, ' ex prima pensione admovit ad nares, suscitans *num odore offenderetur?* et illo negante, atqui, inquit, e lotio est.'"—(Bliss.) [Vespatian took a coin from the first income from the tax and held it to his nose, asking him whether he was really offended by the odour. When he said that he was not, " And yet," said Vespatian, " it is from urine."]

LEST THE CARCASS SHOULD BLEED: it was a common superstition at this time that the body of a murdered man would begin to bleed in the presence of the murderer. The incompetent physician is afraid to await the actual death of his patients, lest he should be convicted of murder by the bleeding of the body in his presence.

ANATOMIES: dissections of bodies, performed as practical demonstrations before students. *Cf.* Jonson, *Every Man in his Humour*, IV., vi.: " They must ha' dissected, and made an Anatomy o' me.'" Marvell: "As if a man should dissect his own body and read the Anatomy lecture." The word was also popularly used of skeletons. The word " skeleton " is not found in Shakespeare.

PROPER: handsome.

PATIENT: the double meaning is one of the stylistic devices of this *genre*.

SMATCH AT: smattering of.

ALCHEMY: as a science alchemy is the precursor of modern chemistry. It had also, however, a complex metaphysical character, which was allied with Hermetic philosophy. In the Middle Ages it was the serious pursuit of the leading scholars and divines and was generally accepted as the most perfect achievement of knowledge. By the seventeenth century it had degenerated into disrepute.

The main concern of alchemy, theoretically and practically, was the transmutation of metals. The search of alchemists was directed towards the discovery of a compound (termed the " Philosopher's stone ") which was thought to have the property of transmuting the baser metals into gold.

MOUNTEBANK: a vagrant dealer in quack medicines. It is uncertain at what period the mountebank appeared in this country, but during the seventeenth and eighteenth centuries he drove a flourishing trade both in town and in country. The mountebank made use of jugglery and tumbling performances to assist his trade and was usually accompanied by a " bourdour " or clown. Their impudence and charlatanism are frequently ridiculed. An amusing paper in the *Spectator* (Vol. VIII., No. 572), shows that their methods were neither different from nor less successful than those of their modern descendants. Compare Butler's Character of *A Mountebank*: " Is an epidemic physician, a doctor-errant, that keeps himself up by being, like a top, in motion, for if he should settle he would fall to nothing immediately. He is a pedlar of medicines, a petty chapman of cures, and tinker empirical to the body of man. He strolls about to markets and fairs, where he mounts on the top of his shop, that is his bank, and publishes his medicines as universal as himself; for everything is for all diseases, as himself is of all places —that is to say, of none. His business is to show tricks and impudence."

GOOD WOMAN: this is clearly the same as the more common " wise woman," that is a woman skilled in popular remedies and herbalism. It is also used of a midwife.

6. A MERE EMPTY WIT.
Page 17.

ON THE STOCK: from his capital.

THIS FIRE OF WIT: at this period we frequently find " this " used where to-day we should use the definite article. This usage is most common in cases where a species is marked off within a wider class—as here " fire *of wit* " is differentiated from fire in general. The use is chiefly found in figurative phrases but is not confined to them. Several instances of this idiom are noted later.

CONCEIT: witticism.

BATES OF: makes a reduction in.

SENSIBLE: perceptible.

MARTIAL: (about 40-102 A.D.). A Roman poet, born at Bilbilis in Spain, the creator of the modern epigram and the first poet to cultivate the epigram as a separate branch of literature. His collection of epigrams is still unsurpassed.

7. A MERE ALDERMAN.
Page 18.

" The Aldermen were the direct representatives of the twenty-six wards (of London), elected for life by the inhabitants; and from their number one was elected annually as Lord Mayor, the chief officer of the City, who, within its bounds, took precedence then as now of all save the king."—(Byrne, *Elizabethan Life*.)

BODY . . . CORPORATION: the pun here derives from the two meanings of " body "—*person* and *public body*. So far as I know, " corporation " had not at this time the meaning " pot-belly." That mode of satire is, however, introduced in the fifth sentence.

SCALE: the reference is to the personification of Justice as a female figure carrying a pair of scales.

WELL-FURNISHED: *i.e.* with drink.

DOOR-POSTS: Municipal notices were affixed to two posts before the house of the Lord Mayor. These were renovated when he entered upon his term of office.

8. A DISCONTENTED MAN.

Page 19.

TAKES PET: sulks.

ACCUSTOMED TENDERNESS: habitual sensitiveness.

HATBAND: the hatband is one of the most enduring articles of male costume. In Edward IV.'s reign a long black band was attached to the hat and going round the neck hung down the back and ended in tassels or a fringe. It enabled the hat either to be worn on the head or thrown back on the left shoulder. This is descended from the *liripipes* or *tippets* frequently seen on brasses of the period. The ordinary hatband, from this time onwards, was worn as the band of the " trilby." It was common among the gallants and gentry to attach large feathers to it. In James I.'s time the hatband became one of the main affectations of the gallant. Hatbands were often elaborately decorated with jewels, and diamond hatbands are mentioned as worn by the Duke of Buckingham. The hatband was sometimes a swathe of silk rolled round the bottom of the crown (the original form of the hatband). This style is mentioned in *Every Man out of his Humour* (1599): " I had a gold cable hatband, then new come up, . . . it was massie goldsmith's work." Thus at the time when Earle was writing a neglected hatband in fashionable circles meant no less than the absence of collar and tie would mean to a well dressed City clerk to-day. Compare *As You Like It*, III. ii. 397: " Your hose should be ungartered, your *bonnet unbanded*, your sleeves unbuttoned, your shoes untied, and everything about you demonstrating a careless desolation."

STILL: throughout the writings of this period " still " is habitually used where we use " always " or " continually." This meaning is more common in the *Characters* than the modern meaning.

GIRDING: sneering at; abusing.

MELANCHOLY: compare Overbury, *Character of a Melancholy Man:* " Is a strayer from the drove: one that nature made sociable, because she made him man, and a crazed disposition hath altered." And *A Distaster of the Time:*

" His blood is of a yellowish colour, like those that have been bitten by vipers, and this gall flows as thick in him as oil in a poisoned stomach."

9. AN ANTIQUARY.
Page 20.

In our own day, for the first time in history, archaeology is pursued as a scientific study. No longer the amusement of some few isolated and exceptional characters, it has become an accepted province of learning, a recognised and reputable field of research at the Universities, and a matter of interest to the educated public. This also is symptomatic of the times. As is proved by the possibility of such an attack as Wilenski's *The Meaning of Modern Sculpture* and fully documented by the archaeological literature, the enthusiasm for archaeology is primarily and almost solely a passion for the acquisition of facts and does not necessarily or often involve an interest in or intelligent appreciation of the value of archaeological discovery, in art or in other fields, for modern civilisation. The study of history and of literature tends more and more to prefer the assembling and manipulation of factual minutiae above the estimation of comparative values. Studies which could logically be justified only as a *means*, if by holding up before us the values and achievements of the past they pointed their relevance to the problems and aspirations which confront us to-day, are pursued blatantly and unquestioned as *ends* with no purpose or justification outside themselves. As many books are written about the unknown details of Shakespeare's life as about the literary value of his works for the modern world.

In face of this symptom Earle's *Character* may have application not only to a type more common now than ever before, but to a general tendency subtly permeating the scholarship of our age. For scholarship is no longer in practical touch with the living movements of the time.

An antiquary is a man who is interested in relics of the past simply because they are past, and whose interest varies inversely with their relevance to the present. The uncritical worship of the past, and uninformed scholarship in things past, are as pernicious as that opposite extreme of our day, the contemptuous neglect of tradition.

ENEMY . . . MAW: " his " means " its," as not infre-
quently at this time: " maw " means " stomach." The
antiquary is an *enemy* of the maw of the past because he
drags things to light which the past has, as it were, digested.

SHEKELS: a shekel was the chief silver coin of the
Hebrews.

PICTURES: *i.e.* on coins. He is more wealthy in old
Roman coins than in current money.

PRINTED BOOKS: the art of printing from movable type
originated in Europe about 1440 A.D. The earliest centre
of printing was Mainz, where Johann Gutenberg had his
press. The first English printer was William Caxton, who
set up a press in Westminster in 1476.

TULLY: Marcus Tullius Cicero (106-43 B.C.). The use
of the name " Tully," which was regular until quite recent
times, is a mark of the pleasant familiarity with the classics
which has now been entirely lost.

PICK . . . BREECHES: *i.e.* his breeches are out of fashion
as a criticism of his own age.

10. A DRUNKARD.

Page 21.

The large increase of drunkenness about the beginning
of the seventeenth century was due in great part to the
changing character of drinks. " Before the end of the
fifteenth century wine had been relatively scarce in England,
and most of what was drunk was native or French, not
very strong in itself and usually diluted with water; while
the ' ale ' used at the medieval festivities . . . was probably
a weak brew made from various kinds of corn, and always
drunk new and unfermented. But during the course of the
sixteenth or early seventeenth centuries all this was changed.
Imported wines became very much more plentiful as English
commerce and naval power expanded; and the fashion
turned, especially after the conclusion of the peace with
Spain in 1604, to the stronger Spanish and Canary wines
which were used for ' sacke.' And a little earlier the
character of ' ale ' had been completely altered by the
introduction of hops from Artois, the use of which spread
pretty rapidly in England after 1525:—

> Hops, Reformation, Carp, and Beer,
> Came into England all in one year.

The new drink was called beer, though after 1600 the terms beer and ale became practically interchangeable as the drinking of ale proper, brewed without hops, disappeared. ... The result, of course, was a deplorable increase of drunkenness all over the country."—R. F. Bretherton, "Country Inns and Alehouses" (in *Englishmen at Rest and Play*).

FENCELESS: defenceless.

CHAM: see Genesis, ix. 22.

HUMOURS: a play upon (*a*) the fluids of the body ; (*b*) states of mind.

11. A YOUNGER BROTHER.
Page 23.

ESAU ... HEELS: see Genesis, xxv. 25-6.

STRAW: the Pharaoh of the oppression (probably Rameses II.), wishing to increase the burdens of the Israelites and dismayed at their prolific increase, enjoined the taskmasters to refuse them straw and yet to require from them the same tale of bricks. This is represented (Exodus, v. 7) as the culmination of his policy of suppression. Petrie, however, is of the opinion that it involved no real hardship.

LIVERIES: livery-servants.

CROOKED ... TYBURN: *i.e.* became highwaymen. The main roads were technically the property of the Crown and specially protected by the King's Peace. The bad state of the highways at this period made travelling difficult, and the prevalence of highway robbery made it dangerous. "Vizard" refers to the mask with which highwaymen concealed their features. Tyburn was a place of execution from the end of the twelfth century; the last execution there took place in 1783. Executions were at this time a popular spectacle, and Tyburn had something of the same sort of public renown as the Paris Garden (*cf.* p. 169).

LOW COUNTRIES: "The Low-countries appear to have afforded ample room for ridicule at all times. In *A brief Character of the Low-countries under the States, being Three Weeks Observation of the Vices and Virtues of the Inhabitants*, written by Owen Felltham, and printed Lond. 1659, 12mo. we find them epitomized as a general sea-land—the great bog of Europe—an universal quagmire —in short, a green cheese in pickle. The sailors (in which denomination the author appears to include all the natives), he describes as being able to ' drink, rail, swear, niggle, steal, and be *lowsie* alike.' Page 40."—(Bliss.) In the Overbury collection there are amusing Characters of *A Drunken Dutchman Resident in England* and of *A Button-Maker of Amsterdam*. Flecknoe has a Character of *A Dutch Wagonner*.

ART . . . BLOOD: his birth enables him to catch some rich and ambitious widow, for by marrying her he can make her a " Gentlewoman."

KENT: *Gavelkind*, or the practice of dividing lands equally among all the male children of the deceased, was (according to Spelman), adopted by the Saxons, from Germany, and is noticed by Tacitus in his description of that nation. *Gloss. Archaiol.* folio, Lond 1664. Harrison, in *The Description of England*, prefixed to Holinshed's *Chronicle* (Vol. I., p. 180), says: " Gavell kind is all male children equallie to inherit, and is continued to this daie in *Kent*, where it is onelie to my knowledge reteined, and no where else in England." And Lambarde, in his *Customes of Kent*, (*Perambulation*, 4to. 1596, p. 538), thus notices it: " The custom of Gavelkynde is generall, and spreadeth itselfe throughout the whole shyre, into all landes subject by auncient tenure unto the same, such places only excepted, where it is altered by acte of parleament."—(Bliss.)

12. A MERE FORMAL MAN.
Page 24.

FORMAL: Butler, in his Character of *An Affected or Formal Man*, uses the words synonymously, but Earle distinguishes them.

FRAME: we still use " frame of *mind*," meaning state or disposition.

GOOD QUIET SUBJECT: " wholly under his control" (ironic). Or, perhaps, " docile to the state."

MANGLING: an ironic expression for " carving."

NEWS . . . WALK: cf. *St. Paul's Walk*, No. 61.

THAT HE WILL . . . NOTHING: the transference of " say " from the earlier position after " will," which would be natural in modern prose, is a very characteristic feature of this style of writing. It must be remembered that the *terse* prose style is yet in its infancy, and ellipsis is still largely experimental.

CHURCH WALK: the first edition has "Minster-walk."

13. A CHURCH PAPIST.
Page 25.

The Act of Uniformity of 1559 imposed fines on all who failed to attend their parish churches. The Catholics were by no means disloyal; their utmost wish was that the Queen would tolerate their worship, or at any rate that the Pope would connive at their attendance of the English services. But the Papal Bull of 1570, excommunicating the Queen and absolving her subjects from their oaths to her, placed them in a cruel dilemma; henceforth "every catholic was forbidden to be a loyal subject." After 1580 a new type of Catholicism penetrated England—that of the Counter-Reformation and the Jesuits, which "generally contained more sedition than religion." Thus in James I.'s reign there were two distinct classes of Catholics— those who were loyal and only troubled by scruples of conscience, and a gang of plotters. Following upon the Gunpowder Plot a new statute (1608) required recusants in addition to their attendance at services to communicate once a year. The fine for failing to do this was £20 a month.

Earle describes sarcastically the catholic who attends service only in order to save his pocket.

APPARITOR: the official of the ecclesiastical or civil court whose duty was to detect and summon offenders to trial.

Overbury says of an Apparitor: "He is a cunning hunter, uncoupling his intelligencing hounds under hedges, in thickets and cornfields, who follow the chase to city suburbs, where often his game is at covert; his quiver hangs by his side stuffed with silver arrows, which he shoots against church-gates and private men's doors, to the hazard of their purses and credit. There went but a pair of shears between him and the pursuivant of hell, for they both delight in sin, grow rich by it, and are by justice appointed to punish it . . ."

HIS MAIN POLICY . . . EASTER: The third rubric prefixed to the Communion Service directs the curate not to suffer

" those betwixt whom he perceiveth malice and hatred to reign . . . to be partakers of the Lord's Table, until he know them to be reconciled." The Church Papist invents some quarrel that it may serve as an excuse for not communicating, and so he can save his conscience without confessing himself a Papist. But, says Earle, his only quarrel is with the Communion itself. Easter is one of the three occasions on which it is enjoined that every parishioner shall communicate.

BATES . . . RELIGION: he reduces her in pin-money what she costs him in religion.

SPINOLA: a Spanish general (1569-1630), of noble Genoese family. He conducted the war in Flanders on behalf of the Spanish government. By his capture of Ostend (1604) he won high reputation. He was apparently expected by English Papists to cross the channel as the protagonist of Rome.

14. A PRISON.
Page 26.

Prison, Prisoner, Jailor, Creditor, etc., are, curiously enough, favourite subjects with the writers of Charactery. There are Characters of A Prison, A Prisoner, A Creditor, A Sergeant, His Yeoman, A Common Cruel Jailor, in the Overbury collection. Perhaps the earliest venture in this field was a pathetic little book by Geffray Mynshul, entitled *Essayes and Characters of a Prison and Prisoners*, written in the King's Bench Prison in Southwark, in 1617.

With this *Character* may be compared Dickens's picture of a debtor's prison, in the Pickwick Papers.

PLUTO'S COURT . . . FANCY: the mythological picture of Pluto's court in Hades was modelled upon the reality of a prison. The anachronism of this conceit detracts nothing from its effectiveness.

MENIPPUS IN LUCIAN: *Lucian* was a Greek writer of rhetorical and satirical works, who flourished in the second century A.D. In his satirical works, which are mostly in dialogue form, he attacks the false culture and lack of taste of his contemporaries. There is scarcely a side of the literary, religious, and social life of his time the absurdities of which he does not present with keen penetration and brilliant humour.

Menippus was a Greek philosopher and cynic (*circa* 250 B.C.), whose writings are lost. He satirised the follies of mankind and especially of philosophers, and was a precursor of Varro and Lucian himself.

The present reference is to Lucian's dialogue *Menippos or Necromancy*, in which Menippus is the chief character. Under the guidance of a Babylonian Magus Menippus visits Hades and gives the following account of it: " But to differentiate each one was no easy task. For they all looked absolutely alike with the bones bare of covering. But with great difficulty and after gazing at them a long while we were able to recognise them ... Many skeletons lay tumbled together and all alike looked forth with a gruesome and vacant stare and showed their bared teeth, so that I was at a loss how to discriminate Thersites from handsome Nireus or Irus from the king of the Phaeacians, or Pyrrhias the sorcerer from Agamemnon."

Thersites was the foul-mouthed demagogue of the Greeks in the Trojan War, who was chastised by Odysseus. Homer says of him: " He was the ugliest man who came to Troy; bandy-legged, lame in his left foot, hump backed, and pigeon chested. His head tapered to a point and was covered by a thin coat of fluffy hair."—(*Iliad*, II. 216-19.) *Nireus* was, after Achilles, the most handsome of the Greeks. *Irus* was the impudent and voracious beggar in Odysseus' house in Ithaca, who insulted him before the suitors when he returned home in the guise of a beggar. The *Knight* must allude to Alcinous, the wise king of the Phaeacians, who harboured Odysseus when cast up upon his land and sent him safely home to Ithaca.

15. A SELF-CONCEITED MAN.
Page 27.

SELF-CONCEITED: the original form of " conceited." Originally " conceited " merely meant " having a (good) opinion of."

EVERY PLACE ... THEATRE: every company his audience.

TENENT: tenet. Both words are from the Latin *tenere* —to hold. " Tenent " is third person plural, " tenet " is third person singular.

ARMINIAN: Jakob van Herman (1560-1609), a man of noble and blameless life, and a brilliant controversalist, professor of theology at Leyden, was the founder of the doctrine which took his name. Arminianism is a mediating protestant system, which attacks the extreme tenets of Calvinism.

In England Andrews and other Cambridge divines formed a growing body of Arminians, but never became dominant. " James himself also was a Calvinist, and sent English divines to take part in the Synod of Dort, a sort of Protestant General Council held in 1619, which condemned Arminianism. On the continent persecution followed; in England, James approved of the decision of the Synod, yet a swift reaction followed . . . In a couple of years the Court had swung round to Arminianism."— (Gwatkin, *Church and State in England to the Death of Queen Anne*, p. 279.)

RAMUS: Petrus Ramus (Pierre de la Ramée) was born in 1515 and murdered during the night of St. Bartholomew, 1572, at the instigation of his scholastic opponent, Charpentier. He was one of the leaders of the Humanistic revolt from scholastic Aristotelianism and attacked not only scholasticism but the dialectical doctrine of Aristotle himself. The controversy had reverberations in Cambridge, where Ramus was attacked by Everard Digby in 1579 and defended by William Temple in 1580 and 1584. Ramus endeavoured, in conscious imitation of Cicero and Quintilian, to blend logic and rhetoric.

PARACELSUS: (born 1493 at Einsiedeln in Switzerland, and died at Salzburg in 1541). Like Ramus he opposed the traditional doctrines of scholasticism. He intended to reform the science of medicine. And as Galen was to Medieval medicine what Aristotle was to Medieval philosophy he was chiefly opposed to Galen. His writings are filled with a curious blend of theosophy and mysticism. The main principle of his medicine was the healing of diseases by the excitation and invigoration of the vital principle against the principle of disease rather than by direct attack upon disease. He vaguely anticipated the doctrine of homoeopathy.

AND LIPSIUS . . . QUINTILIAN: these words are found only in the first edition in place of the preceding clause " and whosoever . . . commended."

JUSTUS LIPSIUS (1547-1606), made an attempt to revive the doctrines of Stoicism at the beginning of the Humanist revival. He introduced a terse and concise Latin style, which found many followers in Germany but which was generally reprobated.

TULLY: Cicero has always been considered the greatest master of Latin rhetorical style.

QUINTILIAN (Marcus Fabius Quintilianus) was born about 35 A.D. at Calagurris in Spain. He practised successfully in Rome and opened a school of rhetoric in Rome during Vespasian's reign. His treatise *De Institutione Oratoria* is extant. In it he outlines the complete course of training in rhetoric and describes the perfect orator. His ideal and model was Cicero. Quintilian was formerly held in higher respect than latterly.

These three comparisons are intended to demonstrate the paradoxical preference of the new-fangled and revolutionary over the stable and generally accepted authority.

16. A SERVING MAN.
Page 29.

IN QUERPO: *Cuerpo* in Spanish means "body" and *in cuerpo* means "in body clothing." Thus the phrase means in undress, or in light jacket without cloak. *Cf.* Beaumont and Fletcher, *Love's Cure*, Act II., Scene i. "By my cloak and rapier, it fits not a gentleman of my rank to walk the streets in querpo." The meaning is here that a gentleman is but half dressed without his lackey.

GOOD LEG: this may be a reference to "running footmen." It was an affectation of the gallants of the time to employ footmen to run before their horses. Overbury has a humorous character of such a footman. Or it may mean "elegant bow," *cf.* p. 49.

CUT: fashion; style. Compare the phrase "a cut above."

HANDSOME: smart.

HAWKING AND HORSE-RACE TERMS: Hawking was originally a favourite sport of the nobility, Edward III. being, according to Froissart, fanatically addicted to it. Strutt (*Sports and Pastimes*) says: "Persons of high rank rarely appeared without their dogs and their hawks ... These birds were considered as ensigns of nobility; and no action could be reckoned more dishonourable to a man of rank than to give up his hawk." Owing to the diffusion of wealth in Elizabeth's reign the sport was more popularly practised. In *Every Man in his Humour* (I. i. 44) Master Stephen, the Country Gull, says, "An a man have not skill in the hawking and hunting languages now-a-days, I'll not give a rush for him."—(Quoted by West.) In his *Itinerary* (1598) Hentzner says that hawking was the general sport of the English nobility. It was at the zenith of its popularity at the beginning of the seventeenth century. It declined rapidly with the advent of the musket, and by the end of the century was almost unknown. An elaborate technical vocabulary was developed in connection with the sport and dropped out of use with its decline.

The first mention of horse-racing is, according to Strutt, in a description of London by Fitzstephen, who lived in Henry II.'s reign. Until well on into the seventeenth century horse-racing was a liberal sport, unconnected with betting, and ranked with hawking and hunting. By the middle of the century horse-races had become a mischievous source of extravagance. Strutt quotes Burton (*Anatomy of Melancholy*, Part II., Sec. 2, Ch. 4, 1660): " Horse-races are desports of great men, and good in themselves, though many gentlemen by such means gallop quite out of their fortunes." A still clearer indication is found in a Character of a Horse-Race by Donald Lupton, in *London and Country Carbonadoed* (1632). Yet the mischief was due primarily to extravagance in the purchase of costly thoroughbreds. There is no clear indication of gambling until the following century. Strutt quotes a ballad from *Pills to Purge Melancholy* (1719) by Henry Parrot, in which betting at horse-races is mentioned together with betting at dice, cock fights, etc.

THE BEST WORK . . . DOES HIM: *i.e.* the master marries his cast-off mistress to his valet. A similar joke appears in Overbury's Character of a *Serving Man*.

17. A TOO IDLY RESERVED MAN.

Page 30.

MACHIAVELLI: Nicolo Machiavelli (1469-1527), was the son of a Florentine lawyer. He held office under the free Republic of Florence, 1494-1512, but was banished on the return of the Medici. He retired to his small property at San Casciano, where he devoted himself to the literary works which have caused his name to endure. Owing to general misunderstanding of the doctrines of *The Prince*, his most famous work, his name has become synonymous with unscrupulous duplicity. His translator, W. K. Marriott, writes: " While it is idle to protest against the world-wide and evil signification of his name, it may be pointed out that the harsh construction of his doctrine

which this sinister reputation implies was unknown to his
own day, and that the researches of recent times have
enabled us to interpret him more reasonably."

STINKING: this word, now only used vulgarly, was very
common as an expression of disgust from the fourteenth
to seventeenth centuries.

LETTERS: *i.e.* private and personal letters.

PRIMIVIST: " Primivist and primero were, in all proba-
bility, the same game, although Minshew, in his Dictionary,
calls them ' *two* games at cardes.' . . . The coincidence
between Mr. Strutt's description of the former and the
passage in the text shews that there could be little or no
difference between the value of the cards in these games,
or in the manner of playing them. ' Each player had four
cards dealt to him, one by one, the *seven* was the highest
card, in point of number, that he could avail himself of,
which counted for twenty-one, the *six* counted for *sixteen*,
the five for fifteen, and the ace for the same,' etc. (*Sports
and Pastimes*, 247.)"—(Bliss.) Mr. West points out that
Primivist and Primero are also mentioned as distinct by
John Taylor, the Water Poet, in the *Motto* (1622). The
evidence seems, on the whole, to indicate that the games,
though closely allied, were distinct. In his edition of
Strutt's *Sports and Pastimes* (1903), Mr. J. Charles Cox,
LL.D., F.S.A., while omitting the above quoted description
of Primivist, asserts, without deigning to mention his
authorities, that Primero was played with *six* cards (p. 263).
He also says: " Queen Elizabeth was fond of taking a
hand at *Primero* which was then the fashionable game of
cards. The favourite game of James I. was *Maw* which
took the place of Primero during his reign; it afterwards
became popular under the name of Five Cards." The
popularity of *Primero* among the nobility is sufficiently
evidenced by the following quotations given by Bliss:—

> —" I left him (Henry VIII.) at Primero
> 　With the duke of Suffolk."—
> 　　　　　　　　　(Shakespeare: *Henry VIII.*)

" Talke of none but lords and such ladies with whom
you have plaid Primero."—(Dekker, *Gul's Hornebooke*,
1609.) That it did not cease to be popular with the
accession of James I. is evidenced by its frequent occurrence
in the literature of the period, both elsewhere and in the
books of Charactery.

The point of the allusion here is that the words of the
" Too Idly Reserved Man " bear no more close relation to

his real meaning or beliefs than the face value of the cards
bears to their counted value in Primivist.

THEY MEAN FREELY: their meaning is guileless.

OEDIPUSSES: solvers of the riddle of his personality.
According to the form of the Oedipus legend adopted by
the tragedians Aeschylus and Sophocles, Oedipus, son of
Laius and Jocasta, frees the city of Thebes from plague by
solving the riddle of the Sphinx. The riddle was: "What
walks on four legs in the morning, on two at noon, and on
three in the evening?" Oedipus correctly explained the
riddle as referring to man in infancy, the prime of life, and
old age.

HEBREW LETTERS: Hebrew is, of course, written from
right to left.

SPELL HIM BACKWARDS: *i.e.* understand him by contraries.

18. A TAVERN.
Page 31.

DEGREE ... STAIRS: a quibble upon two meanings of
"degree," which was at the time commonly used in the
meaning "step" as well as in its present meaning. Mr.
West renders: "a step, or, if you please, a whole flight of
steps."

"It is clear that three types of houses which sold alco-
holic liquor were recognized [*i.e.* at law]. There was the
Inn, which was primarily a hostelry for travellers, though
of course it also sold wine and beer to the inhabitants of
the district. There was the *Tavern*, or wine-shop, which
seems to have been more especially found in the larger
towns and sea-ports: this specialised in the selling of
wine both for consumption on and for consumption off the
premises, but also usually provided cooked meals, and was
probably the ancestor of the eighteenth-century coffee-
house and the modern restaurant. And finally there was
the *Alehouse*, which was the product mainly of the villages
and smaller towns, and did not in fact provide accom-
modation for travellers save by exception. Naturally, in
practice, the distinction between these different institutions
became blurred; but it still remained important as affecting
the application of the licensing laws and the general status
of the house."—R. F. Bretherton, "Country Inns and
Alehouses" (in *Englishmen at Rest and Play*, by Members
of Wadham College).

With this Character should be read the following Character of *Ale-Houses*, by Donald Lupton:—

"If these houses have a Box-bush, or an old post, it is enough to show their profession. But if they be graced with a sign complete, it's a sign of good custom. In these houses you shall see the *History of Judith, Susannah, Daniel in the Lions' Den*, or *Dives and Lazarus* painted upon the wall. It may be reckoned a wonder to see or find the house empty, for either the parson, churchwarden, or clerk, or all, are doing some church or court-business usually in this place. They thrive best where there are fewest. It is the Host's chiefest pride to be speaking of such a gentleman, or such a gallant that was here, and will be again ere long. Hot weather and thunder, and want of company are the hostess's grief, for then her ale sours. Your drink is usually very young, two days old; her chiefest wealth is seen if she can have one brewing under another. If either the hostess, or her daughter or maid will kiss handsomely at parting, it is a good shooing-horn or bird-lime to draw the company thither again sooner. She must be courteous to all, though not by nature yet by her profession; for she must entertain all, good and bad, tag and rag, cut and long-tail. She suspects tinkers and poor soldiers most; not that they will not drink soundly, but that they will not pay lustily. She must keep touch with three sorts of men: that is, the malt-man, the baker, and the Justice's clerks. She is merry, and half mad, upon Shrove Tuesday, May-days, feast-days, and Morris dances. A good ring of bells in the parish helps her to many a tester. She prays the parson may not be a Puritan. A bag-piper, and a puppet-play brings her in birds that are flush. She defies a wine-tavern as an upstart outlandish fellow, and suspects the wine to be poisoned. Her ale, if new, looks like a misty morning, all thick; well, if her ale be strong, her reckoning right, her house clean, her fire good, her face fair, and the town great or rich, she shall seldom or never sit without chirping birds to bear her company, and at the next Churching or Christening, she is sure to be rid of two or three dozen of cakes and ale by gossiping neighbours."

Wye Saltonstall also has a slighter Character of Country Alehouses.

Finally, the following description of large Inns, existing on the main high roads for the convenience of travellers, completes the tale:—

"The World affords not such inns as England hath,

either for good and cheap entertainment after the guests' own pleasure, or for humble attendance upon passengers; yea even in very poor villages ... For as soon as a passenger comes to an inn, the servants run to him, and one takes his horse and walks him till he be cold, then rubs him and gives him meat, yet I must say that they are not much to be trusted in this last point, without the eyes of the master or his servant to oversee them. Another servant gives the passenger his private chamber, and kindles his fire; the third pulls off his boots, and makes them clean. Then the host or hostess visit him; and if he will eat with the host, or at a common table with others, his meal will cost him sixpence, or in some places but fourpence (yet this course is less honourable and not used by gentlemen); but if he will eat in his own chamber, he commands what meat he will, according to his appetite, and as much as he thinks fit for him and his company, yea the kitchen is open to him, to command the meat to be dressed as he best likes; and when he sits at table, the host or hostess will accompany him, or if they have many guests, will at least visit him, taking it for courtesy to be bid sit down: while he eats, if he have company especially, he shall be offered music, which he may freely take or refuse; and if he be solitary, the Musicians will give him the good day with music in the morning. It is the custom, and no way disgraceful, to send up part of supper for his breakfast. In the evening or in the morning after breakfast, (for the common sort use not to dine, but to ride from breakfast to supper time, yet coming early to the inn for better resting of their horses) he shall have a reckoning in writing, and if it seem unreasonable, the host will satisfy him for the due price, or by abating part, especially if the servant deceive him in any way, which one of experience will soon find ... I will only add, that a gentleman and his man shall spend as much as if he were accompanied with another gentleman and his man; and if gentlemen will in such sort join together to eat at one table, the expense will be much diminished. Lastly, a man cannot more freely command at home in his own house, than he may do in his inn; and at parting, if he give some few pence to the chamberlain and ostler, they wish him a happy journey."

Fynes Moryson, *Itinerary* (1617), Part III., p. 151.

Tavern life became very popular in London in Shakespeare's time, and among the many taverns of London the Mermaid and the Mitre have acquired a permanent place in the history of literature. Thomas Heywood has an amusing rhyming catalogue of London Taverns.

VINTNER'S NOSE: " Enquire out those taverns which are best customd, whose maisters are oftenest drunk, for that confirmes their taste, and that they choose wholesome wines."—Dekker, *Gul's Horne-booke* (1609), quoted by Bliss.

IVY-BUSH: the possession of a *sign* was compulsory by law. In the case of country ale-houses a mere box-bush or pole might suffice (*cf.* Lupton). " In the case of Taverns it was the law, at least in the eighteenth century, that ' every retailer shall cause the word WINE to be expressed in legible characters in some visible place in or near the door . . .'"—(Burn, *Justice of the Peace*, 8th ed., Vol. II., p. 576.) " The larger inns even at the beginning of the period showed large and well wrought signs, either hung out on a pole above the door, or else swinging in a kind of triumphal arch by the roadside. In 1587 Harrison could write: ' Finallie there is not so much omitted among them as gorgeousnes of their verie signs at their doores, wherein some do consume thirtie or fortie pounds, a mere vanitie in my opinion, but so vaine will they needs be, and that not onelie to give some outward token of the inne keepers welth, but also to procure good ghests to the frequenting of their houses in the hope there to be well used'"—(*Description of England*, 2nd ed., 1587, p. 109), R. F. Bretherton, *op. cit.* Compare also the Character of *A Painter:* " If she (*scil.* the hostess of a sooty alehouse) aspire to the conceit of a *sign* and desire to have her *birchpole* pulled down, he will supply her with one . . . A mere-maid, says she, for that will sing catches to the youths of the parish. A lion, says he, for that's the only sign that he can make."—(Clitus Alexandrinus, *Whimzies*, 1631.)

GOOD BRINGING UP: *i.e.* satisfactory bringing up of ale, etc.

HIGH CALLING: *i.e.* being called loudly by the guests. (Both these phrases are puns, the secondary meanings being " up-bringing " and " noble profession.")

THEATRE: place where something may be observed (with allusion to the ordinary meaning).

TRULY ACTED: men's true natures are revealed in their conduct (with allusion to *stage*-acting).

NOT PLAYED: not concealed by the assumption of a false role (with allusion to stage plays).

PLUTARCH: (about 50–120 A.D.). A Greek writer and the tutor of the future emperor Hadrian. His literary reputation is founded chiefly on his *Parallel Lives,* a series of biographies arranged in contrasting pairs. Plutarch's object was not to write history but to portray character by the selection of characteristic traits. He is thus one of the earliest writers to show a marked propensity towards Charactery. But his sketches are spoiled as Characters by his moral preoccupations, which caused him to represent his characters either as models of virtue in general or as wholly swayed by some one passion in particular.

Besides the *Parallel Lives,* 83 writings on various subjects are preserved, and are improperly classed together under the general title *Moralia.* Earle here refers to the *De Inimicorum Utilitate* (Ch. VI. of the *Moralia*), but has muddled his authority. The story is as follows:—

TELEPHUS was the son of Hercules, and fought against the Greeks at Troy. He was wounded in the thigh by Achilles. The wound did not heal and he was told by an oracle that it could only be healed by him who had inflicted it. He obtained possession of Agamemnon's infant son and was thus able to compel Agamemnon to persuade Achilles to heal the wound. Achilles healed it by the rust of the spear which had inflicted it. Plutarch is quite clear that it is Achilles' and not Telephus' spear which healed the wound.

SHERRY: substituted in the sixth edition (1633) for "Canary" of the earlier editions. The two are really identical. Sack, or, as it was originally spelt, *seck,* at first applied only to the dry wines grown in the region of Jerez in Spain. This is Sherry proper. But towards the end of the sixteenth and during the seventeenth century, "sack" came to be used of any wine resembling the wine of Jerez and included those from Canary and Madeira. In the literature of the time Sherry, Sack, Sherry-Sack, Canary, were used indifferently.

> "Two kinsmen neare allyde to Sherry-Sack,
> Sweet Malligo and delicate Canary."
> *(Pasquil's Palinodia,* 1619.)

> "Some Sack, boy
> Good Sherry-Sack, Sir ?
> I meant Canary, Sir; "
> (Haywood and Rowley, *Fortune by Sea and Land,* 1655.)

Markham says: "Your best Sacks are of Jerez in Spain, your smaller of Galicia and Portugal; your strong Sacks are of the islands of the Canaries and Malligo." Howell, however, in a letter to Lord Clifford (1634) considers Canary the best wine. Canary wine has come down to literary fame with the Mermaid Tavern. And "sherris-sack" will be for ever renowned for Falstaff's glorious panegyric upon it (*2 Henry IV.*, IV. iii. 91 ff.). The trade in Canary continued until 1853, when a blight destroyed the vines. But the popularity of Sack, both Spanish and Canary, suffered a temporary eclipse during the first three-quarters of the eighteenth century, giving place, as we learn from Tom Brown (*Works*, Vol. IV., p. 65), to brandy; it returned again to favour under the modern name of Sherry. (For these facts I am indebted to A. L. Simon, *History of the Wine Trade in England*, Vol. III., Ch. 12, and H. Warner Allen, *Romance of Wine*, p. 139.)

19. A SHARK.
Page 32.

SHARK: "A worthless and impecunious person who gains a precarious living by sponging on others, by executing disreputable commissions, cheating at play, and petty swindling; a parasite; a sharper."—(*New English Dictionary*.)

CASHIERED: "cast off."

POTTLE: "tankard."

POINTS: in the sixteenth and seventeenth century laces decorated at the ends with tags were, in the absence of buttons, used in profusion to secure the various parts of the dress—but mainly to keep up the *hose* and at the shoulders. The reference here is of course to the points which secured the hose. The word "hose," which is now used of the long stocking, was at this date used for the part of the dress which corresponded to the modern breeches. In origin breeches are merely the upper part of the stockings which, in Henry VIII.'s reign, and onwards, were worn wide at the top and "bombasted," or stuffed, and slashed. The following quotation is given by Fairholt in his *Costume in England*, and appropriately used here by West:—

> *Falstaff.* Their points being broken—
> *Poins.* Down fell their hose.
>
> (Shakespeare, *1 Henry IV.*, II. iv. 238.)

SUBSIDIES: "parliamentary grants to the sovereign."

DISPEND: "afford."

COMMENDATIONS: "letters of recommendation"; or, "greetings."

AT ELEVEN OF THE CLOCK: in his *Description of England* Harrison has a chapter "Of the food and diet of the English," in which he says: "With us the nobilitie, gentrie, and the students, doo ordinarilie go to dinner at *eleven before noone*, and to supper at five, or between five and six at afternoone." Merchants and labourers dined and supped later. Compare *The Knight of the Burning Pestle*, in which Merrythought says: "I never came into my dining-room, but, at eleven and six o'clock, I found excellent meat and drink o' th' Table."

SHERIFF'S HOSPITALITY: "alluding to the public dinners given by the Sheriff at particular seasons of the year."— (Bliss.)

20. AN INSOLENT MAN.
Page 33.

BATE: reduce; lessen. Chiefly used now in the phrase "bated breath."

GIVE HIM THE PATIENCE OF: be patient under.

IMPUTATION: assumption of merit. The word combines "ostentation" and "self-righteousness." It is a pity that it has dropped out of regular use.

PREFERMENT: advancement.

21. ACQUAINTANCE.
Page 35.

With the ideas of Friendship contained in this Character should be compared the Character of *A Friend* by John Stephens, in *Satyrical Essayes, Characters, and Others* (1615). In the following excerpts, which are worth preserving on their own account, the parallel is particularly striking:—

"He is nearer to me than marriage or natural kindred of the same blood; because love without kindred or ceremony is more to be admired, and by consequent more precious. Marriage or kindred goes oftentimes no further than the name or body: but Friendship is annexed with unanimity . . . His multitude of acquaintance doth not extenuate his love nor divide his affection. . . He is much dearer than my legs and arms, for he is my body and my soul together. His honour is true love: which being so, he loves because he will not, and not because he cannot, alter. . . A Friend therefore must be freely chosen, not painfully created. . . He is manifest to me, whilst invisible to the world . . . A second meeting thinks him fit: a second trial knows him a fit Friend. The mere imagination of a Friend's love is an enchanted armour; my heart is impenetrable whilst I wear the comfort, for whether I survive or die my Friend preserves me. . . ."

FIRST DRAUGHT: preliminary sketch.

THE ORDINARY USE . . . SOCIETY: the ordinary object of acquaintance is " to get rid to some extent of shyness in society."—(West.)

SULLENER: holding aloof.

STAUNCH: *i.e.* they keep up acquaintance longer, not letting it become friendship.

PARTIAL: biased, *cf.* Character No. 56.

ENGAGED: under obligation.

22. A CARRIER.

Page 36.

Before the days of the penny post the carrier was a functionary of considerable importance. In Earle's day the carrying trade was well organised and there were regular services between most of the large towns and London. Among the curiosities of literature are two essays in verse Charactery written by the poet Milton on the death of Thomas Hobson, for sixty years carrier between Cambridge and London.

HIS OWN HACKNEYMAN: a hackneyman is a man who keeps hackney horses (or " hacks ") for hire. The carrier is a hackneyman *of himself*, for he lets himself out at hire.

NO UNLETTERED MAN: *i.e.* he carries letters. A play upon words.

BUDGET: bag or wallet. It was also used for a kind of boot in a carriage for carrying luggage, and may be so used here. The meaning " set of letters " is also suggested.

VAULT IN GLOUCESTER CHURCH: a whispering gallery, mentioned by Sir Robert Atkins in *Ancient and Present state of Glostershire* (1712).

HUMANITY: civility. The *tokens* are the letters he brings from friends.

NO MAN DOMINEERS . . . HORSES: a considerable proportion of the profits of the large inns on the main thoroughfares was derived from the charges for stabling horses. Thus a horse-traveller was certain of welcome while a traveller on foot was less readily received. The carrier, being both mounted and a regular guest, could afford to " give himself airs on the strength of his horses."—(West.)

LOAD: a play upon the meanings *luggage* and *load of drink.*

STILL PACKING AWAY: always taking himself off,—on the move. " Packing " survives in the phrase " to send packing."

23. A MERE COMPLIMENTAL MAN.
Page 37.

The parallel between this Character and Butler's *A Complimenter* is very close, as the following extracts will show. " He is very free in making presents of his services, because he is certain he cannot possibly receive in return less than they are worth. He differs very much from all other critics in punctilios of humour; for he esteems himself very uncivilly dealt with if his vows and protestations pass for anything but mere lies and vanities. When he gives his word he believes it is no longer his, and therefore holds it very unreasonable to give it and keep it too. . . . He extols a man to his face, like those that write in praise of an author to show their own wit, not his whom they undertake to commend. He has certain set forms and routines of speech, which he can say over while he thinks on anything else, as a Catholic does his prayers, and therefore never means what he says . . . He had rather be every man's menial servant than any one man's friend; for servants gain by their masters, and men often lose by their friends."

VIRGIL: Earle alludes to Vergil's account of Aeneas' meeting with the shade of his father Anchises in Hades, in the 6th book of the Aenead, ll. 701-2. " Thrice he vainly enfolded in his arms the ghost, which eluded his grasp, light as the winds and like to a winged dream."

EULOGY: this is emended from "Elogie." At this period "elogy" and "eulogy" are frequently confused. "Elogy" (from Latin *elogium*, an inscription) means a short summary of character. "Eulogy" (from Greek εὐλογια) means "praise." As the former was generally laudatory, the two words came to be used interchangeably.

ABUSES: injures.

24. A POOR FIDDLER.

Page 38.

OUT OF CASE: a verbal play upon (1) *fiddle-case* and (2) *in sorry plight*.

PINED: woe-begone; starved.

JOHN DORY: a popular song of the time. "John Dory" (a corruption of *Doria*, the name of a powerful family of Genoa), a pirate captain, was engaged by the French king John to bring an English crew captive to Paris, but in the attempt to capture an English vessel he was himself taken prisoner by "Nicholl a Cornishman." Such is the burden of the song, the words and tune of which are given in Chappell's *Popular Music of Olden Time*, Vol. I., p. 67. The song is frequently mentioned by writers of the seventeenth century. Beaumont and Fletcher refer to it in *The Knight of the Burning Pestle* and in *The Chances*. It is referred to at the end of the century by Dryden in the following couplet:

> "To be repeated like John Dory,
> When fiddlers sing at feasts."

FAIRS: compare Wye Saltonstall, *A Pretty Country Fair*: "A ballad-singer may be sooner heard here than seen, for instead of the viol he sings to the crowd. If his ballad be of love the country wenches buy it to get by heart at home, and after sing it over their milk-pails." And Clitus Alexandrinus, *A Ballad-Monger*: "He never casts his slough but against Bartholomew Fair."

The seventeenth century was the Golden Age of English music; and that not only at the higher levels of the art, but throughout the country at every festive gathering instrumentalists and ballad singers were in popular demand.

PURITAN: compare Donald Lupton, *Alehouses*, p. 130.

COUNTRY WEDDING: compare Wye Saltonstall, *A Country Bride*. After "her marriage knot is tied," he says, "the fiddlers now crowd on." For "the bride is but the

May-game of a country village, that fills the town with mirth and music."

GOES FOR: is taken as.

OVERLOOKS: looks down on.

BAGPIPE: "An instrument, in one or other of its forms, of very great antiquity. By the Greeks it was named ἀσκαυλος or συμφώνεια; by the Romans *Tibia utricularis*. . . . It appears on a coin of Nero, who, according to Suetonius, was himself a performer upon it. It is mentioned by Procopius as the instrument of war of the Roman infantry. In the crozier given by William of Wykeham to New College, Oxford, in 1403, there is the figure of an angel playing it. Chaucer's miller performed on it—

"A bagpipe well couth he blowe and soune."

Shakespeare often alludes to it."—(Grove, *Dictionary of Music and Musicians*.)

25. A YOUNG MAN.
Page 39.

CONCEIT: fancy.

APPEARING GLISTER: apparent glitter; superficial brilliance.

THIS FANCY: *i.e.* the idea that they constitute happiness.

PROSECUTE THE MOTIONS: further the promptings.

SPENDS IT: "wastes it" is the implied meaning.

DISTATES: disrelishes; regards with aversion.

SAD: gloomy.

INFLAMMATION: fire; ardour.

26. AN OLD COLLEGE BUTLER.
Page 41.

The functions of the College butler at this date apparently included those of the modern head porter and steward. And inasmuch as the discipline was then more minute and extensive than to-day, his duties approximated more closely to those of an usher in a school.

GALLOBELGICUS: a Latin periodical, started in 1598 as an annual periodical and continued after 1605 half-yearly.

KECKERMAN: 1573–1609. A systematiser of various branches of science and philosophy. His works were notorious for their elaborate divisions and subdivisions.

A PRIMO ORTUM: "that which arises from the first (division)." Having divided the loaf into two parts he divides each of these parts (*a primo orta*) into two again, and so on.

NICELY: meticulously.

OVERSEEN: overtaken by drink; drunk.

MANCHET: the finest grade of white bread.

HATCH: buttery hatch.

CUES AND CEES: "Cue" (Q) originally stood for *quadrans*, a farthing. But it was used in the University for ⅛ of a penny, which was the price of a cup of beer. Later it came to be used of the measure of beer which originally cost ⅛ penny. "Cee" (C) was probably derived from the first letter of *cyathus* and represented a small measure either of beer or bread. The origin and use of these terms, so far as they can be retraced, are fully discussed by C. Wordsworth, *Social Life at the English Universities in the Eighteenth Century*, pp. 651 ff.

POST AND PAIR: "an old game of cards, in which the hands consisted of three cards, that hand being the best which contained the highest pair royal, or, if none contained a pair royal, the highest pair."—West.

27. A MEDDLING MAN.
Page 42.

Compare Butler, *A Busy Man*. "Is one that seems to labour in every man's calling but his own, and, like Robin Goodfellow, does every man's drudgery that will let him. He is like an ape, that loves to do whatsoever he sees others do, and is always as busy as a child at play .. He covets his neighbour's business, and his own is to meddle, not do. .... He wonderfully affects to seem full of employments, and borrows men's business only to put it on and appear in, and then returns it back again, only a little worse. He frequents all public places, and, like a pillar in the old Exchange, is hung with all men's business, both public and private, and his own is only to expose them. He dreads nothing so much as to be thought at leisure, though he is never otherwise; for though he is always doing, he never does anything."

LISTEN . . . EARNESTLY: compare Joseph Hall, *Character of a Busybody:* "His ears are long and his eyes quick, but most of all to imperfections, which as he easily sees, so he increases with intermeddling."

ENGAGEMENT: obligation.

28. AN UPSTART COUNTRY KNIGHT.
Page 43.

This is the favourite butt of the Character writers. The purchasing of knighthoods in James I.'s reign is frequently referred to satirically in the literature of the period. In his essay on Thomas Middleton (*Selected Essays*, pp. 161 ff), Mr. T. S. Eliot adopts the thesis of Miss Kathleen Lynch in *The Social Mode of Restoration Comedy*, that "the transition from Elizabethan-Jacobean to later Caroline comedy is primarily economic: that the interest changes from the citizen aping gentry to the citizen become gentry and accepting that code of manners." "Middleton, she observes, marks the transitional stage in which the London tradesman was anxious to cease to be a tradesman and to become a country gentleman." "As a social document the comedy of Middleton illustrates the transition from government by a landed aristocracy to government by a city aristocracy gradually engrossing the land." The Character writers are replete with hints of this social tendency.

"IS A . . . HIMSELF": these words take the place of "His honour . . . preposterous," which are found only in the first edition.

HOLIDAY CLOWN: *cf.* Shakespeare: *Tempest*, II. i.: "Were I in England now, as once I was, and had but this fish painted, not a *holiday* fool there but would give a piece of silver." From the meaning "taking a holiday" the word was employed in a pejorative sense to mean "idler" or "good for nothing."

FOR HE BORE . . . WIELD IT: "Arms" is used in the literal and heraldic senses. West says: "The man had no arms when the king knighted him." But this makes the passage a banal truism of the sort in which Earle does not indulge; "bore the King's sword" refers, I think, to fighting in the king's service.

STOCK: a play upon *capital* and *pedigree*.

GUARDED: edged with braid. The fashion of covering the edges and seams of dresses with gold and silver lace *guards* was prevalent among all classes of society. Thomas Lodge, in his *Euphues golden Legacie* (1592), describes the holiday attire of the countryman as including " hose of grey kersey, with a large slop barred all across the pocket-holes with three fair *guards*, stitched on either side with red thread." Compare Lyly's *Euphues* (1582): " If a tailor make your gown too little, you cover his fault with a broad stomacher; if too great, with a number of pleats; if too short, with a faire *garde*." And Shakespeare, *Merchant of Venice*, II. ii. 163, " Give him a livery more *guarded* than his fellows'." The fashion persists in the modern court dress.

DOGS: hunting has always been a favourite and privileged sport in England. Strabo tells us that the dogs bred by the ancient Britons were highly prized on the Continent because of their excellence for hunting. In Saxon and still more in Norman times the hunting laws were oppressive to the point of tyranny upon the common people. James I. was a fanatical devotee of the sport. In *The King's Christian Duties*, which he wrote for the instruction of his son, he says: " I cannot omit hare hunting, namely with running hounds, which is the most honourable and noblest thereof." Thus, then as now, a kennel was among the first preoccupations of the parvenu. In his Character of *A Gentleman's House in the Country* Wye Saltonstall says: " All the rooms smell of dogs and hawks."

A HAWK . . . NOBILITY: *cf.* p. 126.

JESSES: " All hawks taken upon ' the fist,' the term used for carrying them upon the hand, had straps of leather called jesses, put about their legs. The jesses were made sufficiently long for the knots to appear between the middle and the little fingers of the hand that held them, so that the lunes, or small thongs of leather might be fastened to them with two tyrrits, or rings; and the lunes were loosely wound round the little finger. It appears that sometimes the jesses were of silk."—(Strutt, *Sports and Pastimes.*)

HUNTERS: grooms.

RACE: (1) career; (2) family.

RETURN . . . CAME: the words of the death sentence. This is a pun, the intended meaning being " return to their plebeian status."

29. A GOOD OLD MAN.
Page 44.

NEXT DOOR: how much more vivid is this than " extreme nearness " or " proximity " !

EXPECTS: awaits.

PRACTISES HIS EXPERIENCE ON: influences by his experience.

HE HAS SOME . . . : contrast *An Old Man*, by Wye Saltonstall: " His memory is full of the actions of his youth, which he often histories to others in tedious tales, and thinks they should please others because himself." Nowhere is Earle's superiority more pronounced than in this sympathetic portraiture of old age, in contrast with the ruthless ridicule of Overbury's and Saltonstall's Characters.

CATO: " A collection of 146 proverbs, each in a couple of hexameters. This book belongs to the later Empire, though it is probably not later than the end of the fourth century A.D. It was a well-known manual in the Middle Ages, and was widely circulated in translations."—(Seyffert and Nettleship, *Dictionary of Classical Antiquities*.) In the sixteenth century this book was confounded with the prose *Praecepta ad Filium* of Cato the Censor (243-149 B.C.), which is not extant.

PUT THE BOY (FOOL) ON: treat as a boy (fool).

CREDITS: reflects credit on.

30. AN IDLE GALLANT.
Page 46.

The artificial, be-padded and be-frilled costume that developed in Elizabeth's reign was not in the least modified by the accession of James I. What had been gaiety in Elizabeth's reign became mere frivolity in that of James. The vanity, frivolity, and conceit of the gallant or fop at this period are satirised throughout the contemporary literature. The most easily accessible authority is Dekker's *Gul's Horne-booke*.

IDLE: worthless; frivolous.

GALLANT: fashionable beau.

GRATULATES: is thankful or glad at.

BRAVERY: finery. Hebrew mythology places the origin of clothes in the sin of Adam. As the gallant is wholly preoccupied with dress, he is naturally, says Earle, grateful to Adam.

TERMS: the terms of the law-courts. When the Inns of Court played a larger part in the life of London the difference in the life of the town during "terms" was less than, but comparable to, the difference between Oxford or Cambridge to-day in term and in vacation. There was a regular influx of persons at the beginning of the term, bent on business or pleasure. These were called "termers," and it seems likely that this (the reading of the first edition) is the correct reading here. "Observes" means "frequents."

GAMING: in the sixteenth and seventeenth centuries cheating with dice and cards had been reduced to a fine art. In *The Belman of London* (1608) Dekker enumerates fourteen different kinds of false dice. The falsity of dices and of dicers' oaths had become a byword. *Cf.* Shakespeare, *Winter's Tale*, I. ii. 133, "false as dice are to be wished by one that fixes No bourn 'twixt his and mine"; and *Hamlet*, III. iv. 45, "as false as dicers' oaths." Mr. A. Forbes Sieveking says (*Shakespeare's England*, Vol. II., p. 454), "it is an undoubted fact that in Tudor days we derived our recreations and pastimes, as we did our intellectual culture and refinements, from Spanish, Italian, and French sources." Foreign oaths were introduced as the latest fashion in connection with games derived ultimately from abroad.

PICKTOOTH: "Toothpicks, introduced from abroad, were much in request. These when treated as trinkets were often of gold and highly ornamented; many such are mentioned among the Queen's gifts. In *King John*, I. i. 189-92, the Bastard says:

'Now your traveller,
He and his toothpick at your worship's mess,
And when my knightly stomach is suffic'd,
Why then I suck my teeth;'

and Benedict in *Much Ado* (II. i. 276-7):

'I will fetch you a toothpicker now from the furthest inch of Asia.'"—(Percy Macquoid, in *Shakespeare's England*, Vol. II., p. 142.) In James I.'s reign toothpicks worn on the person were a symbol of the fop. In Massinger's *Grand Duke of Florence* (1636): "My case of toothpicks and my silver fork" are among the articles of dress which make up "a signior." In Beaumont and Fletcher's *Woman Hater* (1607) "A toothpick in a riband" is mentioned. Also in *All's Well that Ends Well* Parolles says: " the brooch and the toothpick which wear not now."

STARCHED AS HIS LINEN: The upper part of a dandy's figure was encased in a long-waisted doublet, padded and quilted, beneath which stays were frequently worn. Henry Fitzgeffery in *Notes from Black Fryers* (1617) describes the " spruse coxcombe " as having " Whalebone bodies, for the better grace." Starch was introduced in the reign of Elizabeth when long ruffs became the fashion, and the Queen imported Dutch women to teach the art of starching Stubbs (*Anatomie of Abuses*) speaks of " a certain kind of liquid matter which they call starch, wherein the devil hath willed them to wash and die their ruffes well; and this starch they make of divers colors and hues—white, red, blue, purple, and the like; which being drye, will then stand stiff and inflexible about their neckes." The *yellow* starch which became so fashionable was invented by the infamous Mrs. Turner, who was concerned in the murder of Overbury.

RUFFLE ... BOOT: the fashionable gallant wore long boots of very highly polished leather. Earle means that he uses his boots as a looking-glass. Compare 'A Finnical London Citizen' in *Confused Characters of Conceited Coxcombs*, by K.W. (1661) :—" he carries his looking-glass in his shoes, that so whenever he looks down he may correct the rumple in his band."

FELLOW IN BLACK: In Nichol's *Progresses of James I.* (*The Preparation at Oxford*—1605) we learn that " the young Masters of Arts and Batchelors of arts wore ... black wide-sleeved gouns, faced to the foot with taffeta and about the arm to turn up at the elbow, and black civil hoods on the left shoulder."

FIFTY ... POUND: in 1618 the Bakers of London drew up a list of expenses, in which they reckoned £20 a year to clothe man, wife, and two apprentices.

The tendency in Elizabeth's time to adopt various fashions from various countries was exaggerated in James' reign, so that the ordinary dress of the gallant had become a medley of all the countries of Europe. *Cf.* Greene, *Farewell to Folly* (1591): " I have seen an English gentleman so diffused in his suits,—his doublet being for the weare of Castile, his hose for Venise, his hat for France, his cloak for Germanie,—that he seemed no way to be an Englishman but by the face." A similar description is to be found in Dekker's *Gul's Horne-booke* (1609).

31. A CONSTABLE.
Page 47.

DOUBLE JUGS: a *jug* was a measure of beer, a vessel containing about a pint. In *The Knight of the Burning Pestle*, Ralph thanks Squire Tapstero for " comforting our souls with double jug."

32. A FLATTERER.
Page 48.

CASHIERING: dismissal.

BUT . . . DECEIVE HIM: but he associates with him whose fortunes were sufficient to tempt him to take the pains to deceive him.

HUMOURS: moods. *Cf.* p. 120.

JUMP: " jump with " in the sense of " tally " or " coincide " was a much more common expression in the past than it is at present.

POSSESSES: seizes.

EXPECTS: awaits.

33. A DOWNRIGHT SCHOLAR.
Page 49.

Earle writes his University Characters both with more intimate knowledge and more personal interest than most.

CARRIAGE: burden.

IMPRIMIS . . . ITEM: the first edition has " Total "; the meanings are the same.

LEG . . . SCRAPE: a bow made by bending one leg while drawing back the other; *cf.* **35**: " Cleave the ground with hard scraping."

PINS: still used in dialect for " legs "; NICE: used in its correct sense, " elegant," " skilful."

SMACKING: kissing.

VERY WOODCOCK: the woodcock was proverbially foolish.

ONE-AND-THIRTY: a game of cards similar to bone-ace. (*N.E.D.* quotes Florio, 1611, *Trentuno*, a game at cards called one and thirtie, or bone-ace. The game is of the simplest. The third card dealt to each player is turned up and the player who has the highest card wins half the stake or the " bone.")

TABLES: this was a general name for dice games of mixed chance and skill, requiring the use of a board, of which the chief was backgammon.

DOUBLETS: a simpler form of backgammon.

SINISTERLY: a play upon (1) left handedly, (2) awkwardly.

HE CANNOT SPEAK . . . FALCONER: *cf.* p. 126.

34. A HIGH-SPIRITED MAN.
Page 51.

RATE: sum; price (a seventeenth century use).

POSSESS: win.

BATE YOU: let you off.

LAID DOWN WITH SATISFACTION: appeased by an apology.

DEJECT: cast down; humble.

AFTER THOUSANDS: " as though he were worth thousands." For this meaning compare the use of " after " in such phrases as " After (in imitation of) Mr. —, he asserts . . ."; and " after the manner of," etc.

PELTING: paltry; trumpery (archaic).

35. A PLAIN COUNTRY FELLOW.
Page 52.

NEBUCHADNEZZAR: " He was driven from men, and did eat grass as oxen, and his body was wet with the dew of heaven, till his hair was grown like eagles' feathers, and his nails like birds' claws."—(Daniel, iv. 33.)

CONVERSATION: used in the scriptural sense, "way of life."

SALLETS: " salads." Salads, or preparations of raw fruits and vegetables, were coming into fashion among the upper classes, who affected French manners. But the lower classes were still opposed to the innovation.

SUNDAY: Sunday observance was a main point of controversy in the seventeenth century. Within 100 years over 120 books and pamphlets devoted to this subject were published. The movement to greater strictness came, under puritan influence, from the people themselves—" so that the Lords Day, especially in Corporations, began to be precisely kept, people becoming a Law to themselves, forbearing such sports, as yet by statute permitted."— (Fuller.) But in the country villages Sunday remained a day of recreation and enjoyment, as it had been in Catholic England. In the first year of his reign James I. issued a proclamation forbidding bull-baiting, common plays, and all disorderly pastimes on the Sabbath (1603). But in the *Book of Sports* (1618) his attitude seems clearly to be that he wished the people to enjoy " honest recreation " (which included dancing to the pipes) *after divine service.*

CENSURES: sets up as a critic of.

CLOUT: a metaphor from studding the soles of shoes with broad " clout-nails."

WESTMINSTER HALL was rebuilt by Henry II. and the first use to which it was put was the trial of this monarch.

Compare Saltonstall's Character of *A Ploughman*: " The smell of the earth makes him hungry, for he brings home an invincible stomach, and nothing holds him back but a barley pudding. . . . He prays only for a fair seed-time, and of all days will be sure to keep Plough Monday." And compare the ending of this with Earle's: " A good harvest is his happiness, and the last seed he sows is his own body, which he knows like his grain, though it seem to perish, yet shall spring again."

36. A MERE GULL CITIZEN.

Page 54.

An apt parallel to this Character is Beaumont and Fletcher's satire upon the London Citizen in *The Knight of the Burning Pestle.*

GULL: a simpleton.

CLOWN: rustic.

QUALITY: high society.

MINCE: " utter in an affectedly refined manner a complement which does not come suitably from his lips."

IMPUTATION: " making a merit of " a thing.

STOURBRIDGE FAIR: The great fairs, which had existed in England from the early Middle Ages, were the meeting-points of commerce from all the world over. " Sturbridge Fair " was one of the largest and most famous. It covered an area of half a square mile, at Sturbridge outside Cambridge, and lasted for several weeks. From this Fair Bunyan draws his allegory of "Vanity Fair" in the *Pilgrim's Progress*.

FOND PROTESTATION: foolish exclamation.

CHUCK: the absurd language of endearment affected (in imitation of the genteel?) by the citizen class is burlesqued by the language of the Citizen and Wife in *The Knight of the Burning Pestle*.

GOES BETTER OFF ... MAID: makes a better marriage as a widow than she did as a maid. This is in virtue of the wealth she inherits from her first husband, which would enable her to marry out of the class of merchant citizens into the lesser gentry. *Cf.* No. 28 (and note).

HE IS ONE THAT ... CITIZENS: compare the *Induction* of *The Knight of the Burning Pestle*: " Why, present something notably in honour of the commons of the city." A type of bourgeois drama had grown up, celebrating the deeds of famous London citizens, and offering tasteless and exaggerated gratification to the absurd pride of the citizen.

GILDING ... CROSS: " The great cross of West Cheap was originally erected in 1290, by Edward I. in commemoration of the death of Queen Elinor, whose body rested at that place on its journey from Herdeby, in Lincolnshire, to Westminster, for interment. It was rebuilt in 1441, and again in 1484. In 1581 the images and ornaments were destroyed by the populace; and in 1599 the top of the cross was taken down, the timber being rotted within the lead, and fears being entertained as to its safety. By order of Queen Elizabeth, and her privy council, it was repaired in 1600, when, says Stow, ' a cross of timber was framed, set up, covered with lead, *and gilded*,' etc. Stow's *Survey of London*, by Strype, Book III., p. 35, 1720."—(Bliss.)

THE FOUR PRENTICES OF LONDON: a play by Thomas Heywood (1570-1650) especially popular with the citizens of London. It is more fantastic in plot than the most unrestrained of the romances. It is the story of the four sons of the destitute Earl of Boloign, who are bound apprentice in four trades in London. They abandon their trades and proceed to the wars, bearing as devices on their shields the emblems of their respective Companies. After incredibly fantastic adventures they meet at the sack of

Jerusalem. Such is the exaggeration of the play that some critics have thought it was intended as a burlesque upon the popular taste. But Heywood dedicates it seriously "To the honest and high-spirited prentices, the readers." Yet he was not unaware of its faults, for in the Dedication he speaks of it as "written many years since, in my Infancy of Judgement in this kind of Poetry, and my first practice"; and again: "as Playes were then some fifteen or sixteen yeares agoe it was in the fashion."

NINE WORTHIES: of the world, were three pagans, Hector, Alexander, Julius Caesar, three Jews, Joshua, David, Judas Maccabaeus, and three Christians, Arthur, Charlemagne, and Guy of Warwick.

SUFFICIENTER: a play upon the two meanings, (a) substantial, well-to-do, (b) capable, able.

37. A LASCIVIOUS MAN.
Page 55.

SPIRITS: before Harvey's discovery of the circulation of the blood it was believed that blood flowed in the veins and that the arteries contained blood and also "vital spirits" (cf. *Love's Labour's Lost*, IV. iii. 305-6.) This belief continued popularly long after it had been scientifically exploded.

HIS SOUL ... BODY: he employs his higher faculties merely to subserve his physical desires.

PLEAS: excuses.

38. A PLAYER.
Page 57.

Although the age of Elizabeth and James I. marks the period of highest development of the drama in England, and the theatre was patronised as at no other time, the actor was held in very low esteem. By Statute of Elizabeth all actors were social outcasts, ranked with rogues and vagabonds, except those under the patronage of "a Baron of this Realme or any other honourable Personage of greater Degree" or licensed by at least two Justices of the Peace.—(*Act* 16, *Elizabeth, c.* 5, § 5.) *Cf.* Character of *A Player* in *Micrologia* (1629) by R. M. " He often person-

ates a rover and therein comes nearest himself." And
" If he lose one of his fellow-strolls in the summer he
turns king of the gypsies; if not, some great man's protection is a sufficient warrant for his peregrinations and a
means to procure him the Toun Hall." The opponents of
the stage were quick to seize upon this advantage. And
so strong was Puritan opposition, that the development of
drama was successfully inhibited by it.

The difference between the strolling or " common "
player, liable to arrest and classed as a vagabond, and the
licensed actor in the London companies was therefore
great. Except for the exodus occasioned by the several
visitations of the plague, we may say that there was no
decent acting outside London. The many Characters of
the Player agree in tone with Earle's, except only the
following Character of *An Excellent Actor*, in the Overbury
collection.

An Excellent Actor.

Whatsoever is commendable to the grave orator, is most
exquisitely perfect in him; for by a full significant action
of body he charms our attention: sit in a full theatre, and
you will think you see so many lines drawn from the
circumference of so many ears, while the *actor* is the
centre. He doth not strive to make nature monstrous,
she is often seen in the same scene with him, but neither
on stilts nor crutches; and for his voice, 'tis not lower than
the prompter, nor louder than the foil and target. By his
action he fortifies moral precepts with examples; for what
we see him personate, we think truly done before us: a
man of a deep thought might apprehend the ghost of our
ancient heroes walked again, and take him (at several
times) for many of them. He is much affected to painting,
and 'tis a question whether that make him an excellent
player, or his playing an exquisite painter. He adds grace
to the poet's labours: for what in the poet is but ditty, in
him is both ditty and music. He entertains us in the best
leisure of our life, that is between meals, the most unfit
time either for study or bodily exercise. The flight of
hawks and chase of wild beasts, either of them are delights
noble: but some think this sport of men worthier, despite
all calumny. All men have been of his occupation: and
indeed, what he doth feignedly, that do others essentially:
this day one plays a monarch, the next a private person.
Here one acts a tyrant, on the morrow an exile: a parasite
this man to-night, to-morrow a precisian, and so of divers

others. I observe, of all men living, a worthy actor in one kind is the strongest motive of affection that can be: for when he dies, we cannot be persuaded any man can do his parts like him. But to conclude, I value a worthy actor by the corruption of some few of the quality, as I would do gold in the ore; I should not mind the dross, but the purity of the metal.

HE KNOWS . . . AWAY: the comparison of the world to a stage is a commonplace of literature. Saltonstall opens his Character of *The World* with the words: " Is a stage, men the actors." Cf. *As You Like It*, II. vii. 139: " All the world's a stage, And all the men and women merely players."

PAINTING GENTLEWOMEN: painting the face was in vogue in Elizabeth's reign and throughout this century. Like all new devices, it was regarded as a symbol of depravity and vigorously attacked by the Puritanical writers. Saltonstall opens his Character of *A Fine Dame* with: " Is a picture of her own drawing, for most commonly she is painted, and her cheek never alters but keeps one height of colour, which shews it is artificial." For this purpose " Spanish paper " was used. It was made up into little books, and a leaf torn out and rubbed upon the face, neck, or breasts, transferred the vermilion powder with which it was covered. There is some evidence also that the beaus used paint. In Marston's *Antonio and Mellida* (1602) Rossalind says of one of her suitors: " The fifth paints and has always a good colour for what he speaks." And Durfey describes a town gallant " with his paint and his powder and patch."

MASKED . . . GENTLEMAN: compare *A Player* by R. M.: " Sometimes he represents that which in his life he scarce practices—to be an honest man."

RAMPANT: violent.

TIRING HOUSE: dressing room.

INNS OF COURT MEN: Harrison assumes three noble Universities in England, the third being the Inns of Court. " The four Inns of Court—The Middle Temple, the Inner Temple, Lincoln's Inn, Gray's Inn—were at the height of their glory in Elizabeth's reign. Whatever their true origin, it is certain that at that date they formed, along with the more humble Inns of Chancery, a set of colleges for the study of law, linked together (in imitation of the colleges at Oxford and Cambridge) into what would have been a University if they had been incorporated.

The Benchers represented the Master and Fellows of a college, the Utter or Outer Barristers (the Junior Bar of to-day) the Masters of Arts, and the Inner Barristers (now the students) the Batchelors and undergraduates. To make the analogy with Oxford and Cambridge more complete, each Inn of Court had its dining hall, its library, and its chapel; except that the two Temples shared the beautiful old church of the Templars between them. Like a college, too, each Inn was enclosed, and had its garden."—(Arthur Underhill, in *Shakespeare's England*). The Inns of Court men are very frequently mentioned in the drama and social literature of the time, especially in the Characters. Earle mentions them four times. They are usually contrasted as fashionable and idle men of the world with the more serious and superficially less accomplished members of Oxford and Cambridge. The following Character of *An Inns of Court Man*, in the Overbury collection, will be interesting:—

AN INNES OF COURT MAN.

He is distinguished from a scholar by a pair of silk stockings, and a beaver hat, which makes him contemn a scholar as much as a scholar doth a schoolmaster. By that he hath heard one mooting, and seen two plays, he thinks as basely of the University as a young *sophister* doth of the grammar-school. He talks of the University, with that state as if he were her chancellor; finds fault with alterations, and the fall of discipline, with an, *It was not so when I was a student;* although that was within this half year. He will talk ends of Latin, though it be false, with as great confidence as ever Cicero could pronounce an oration, though his best authors for't be taverns and ordinaries. He is as far behind a courtier in his fashion as a scholar is behind him: and the best grace in his behaviour is to forget his acquaintance.

He laughs at every man whose band sits not well, or that hath not a fair shoe-tie, and he is ashamed to be seen in any man's company that wears not his clothes well. His very essence he placeth in his outside, and his chiefest prayer is, that his revenues may hold out for taffeta cloaks in the summer, and velvet in the winter. For his recreation, he had rather go to a citizen's wife than a bawdy house, only to save charges: and he holds fee-tail to be absolutely the best tenure. To his acquaintance he offers two quarts of wine for one he gives. You shall never see him melancholy, but when he wants a new suit, or fears a serjeant: at which times only, he betakes himself to *Ploydon*. By that he hath read *Littleton*, as he can call *Solon*, *Lycurgus*, and *Justinian*, fools, and dares compare his law to a *Lord Chief-Justice's*.

AFTERNOON'S-MEN: tipplers. *Cf.* Burton, *Anat. Melon. Democr. to Reader* (1657), 44: "Beroaldus will have drunkards, afternoon men, and such as more than ordinarily delight in drink, to be mad."—(*N.E.D.*)

SHROVE TUESDAY ... BAWDS: Shrove Tuesday was a great medieval festival and carnival of the Roman Church. This survived in England as a public holiday, which was the particular holiday of the prentices on which they were allowed especial licence. Their two favourite amusements on that day were: (1) "throwing at the cock" (satirized by Hogarth in the first of the prints called the *Four Stages of Cruelty*, and described by Trusler as "the universal Shrove-tide Amusement"); (2) they would visit Turnbull Street, seize so many of the prostitutes as they could lay hold of, and cart them round the town with abuse and ill-treatment. (This is referred to in Donald Lupton's Character of Turnbull Street.) *Cf.* also *The Knight of the Burning Pestle*, V. iii. 170-1:

"Ne'er shall we more upon Shrove Tuesday meet,
And pluck down houses of iniquity."

LENT: Stage performances during Lent were forbidden in 1579 owing to puritan pressure (*cf.* E. K. Chambers, *The Elizabethan Stage*, Vol. IV., p. 278). Bliss quotes Prynne: "There are none so much addicted to stage-playes, but when they goe unto places where they cannot have them, or when, as they are suppressed by public authority, (as in times of pestilence, *and in Lent, till now of late,*) can well subsist without them,"—(*Histrio-Mastix*, 1633).

ACT: see above. The two meanings are played upon (1) Act of a play, (2) Act of Parliament.

CATO: Marcus Porcius Cato (95-46 B.C.), who committed suicide at Utica after Caesar defeated the generals of the Republican party at Thapsus.

39. A DETRACTOR.
Page 58.

We have not the order in which Earle wrote his Characters and he did not himself arrange them for publication.

From the first sentence it appears that this Character was written to follow the Character of *A Suspicious, or Jealous Man*.

MATCH: equal.

MOUNTING: rising to.

RED DRAGON . . . WOMAN: Revelation, xii.

CATCH: criticise; find fault.

SCANDAL: slander or defamation.

INWARD: intimate.

HAVE A SMATCH . . . MALICE: have a touch of his disposition, and what is really malice passes for honest bluntness. (Compare Earle's *Blunt Man*.)

40. A RASH MAN.
Page 59.

SOUGHT TO: consulted.

PICK-THANK: one who steals gratitude he does not deserve (*cf.* pickpocket), hence " sycophant." " Pick-thank " is a character in Bunyan's *Pilgrim's Progress*.

41. A MERE YOUNG GENTLEMAN OF THE UNIVERSITY.
Page 61.

FENCING AND DANCING SCHOOLS: fencing and dancing (*i.e.* dances of *foreign* origin) both became fashionable in Elizabeth's time, and an essential part of a liberal education. The rapier began to take the place of the sword and buckler, and foreign steps of the old English country dances. In the Elizabethan Statutes at Cambridge, fencing and dancing-schools were forbidden alongside of bear or bull-baiting and quoits (chap. 47). Football was also forbidden, yet in his Character of *A Mere Scholar* Overbury says: " the excellency of his College (though but for a match at football) is an article of his faith." The Statutes at the Universities, as the sumptuary laws in the country, were consistently disregarded.

TENNIS: Tennis was played with a small, hard ball and the hand, or a racket, in an enclosed court. It was more akin to Fives than to modern lawn tennis.

BOOKS: " Volumes were formerly placed on the shelves with the leaves, not the back, in front, and the two sides of the binding were joined together with ' neat silk ' or other strings, and in some instances, where the books were of greater value and curiosity than common, even fastened with gold or silver chains."—(Bliss.)

EUPHORMIO: John Barclay (1582-1621), a Scottish writer of great merit. From 1606 to 1616 he lived in London enjoying the favour of James I. as a countryman and a scholar. In 1603 he published his *Satyricon* under the pseudonym " Euphormio Lusinius." This, as the title attests, is based upon the work of Petronius. It is a satirical work, in which he attacks the Jesuits and the Puritans and individuals who were personally obnoxious to him. It obtained a high measure of popularity. His more famous work, the *Argenis*, had not been published when Earle wrote this Character.

GIVES HIM MONEY: in his *Diary* for April 13, 1638, Evelyn says: " My Father order'd that I should begyn to manage myne oun expenses, which till then my Tutor had done; at which I was much satisfied." Wordsworth (*op. cit.*, p. 92) says: " In earlier times the relation between tutor and pupil at the Universities had been similar to that which has of late so happily grown up in higher schools between boy and Master. And indeed the ' *children* ' of the 16th, the ' *boys* ' and the ' *schollers* ' of the 17th, and the ' *lads* ' of the 18th century, differed little in age or discipline from the public schoolboys of the present day."

INGLE . . . HATBANDS: " a hanger-on to noblemen, who are distinguished at the university by gold tassels to their caps."—(Bliss.) *Cp.* " tuft-hunters."

KNIGHT'S SERVICE: the service rendered by a knight, hence " good service." The phrase is used by Thomas Hardy in *Far From the Madding Crowd* (*N.E.D.*)

42. A WEAK MAN.
Page 62.

HUDDLED UP: botched up hastily and badly.

HIS COMPANY . . . BUT INVITED: *i.e.* he is never himself invited into company but must invite others, if he is to have company.

43. A TOBACCO-SELLER.

Page 63.

This is among the slightest of Earle's Characters, and it appears that he did not favour the tobacco habit. Yet so important is this in the social life of the day that a few words of introduction are necessary.

Tobacco was first popularised in Europe by Jean Nicot, about 1560. But it was used for medicinal purposes only. The faith in its medicinal properties was remarkable and persisted even among those who later opposed the practice of smoking. England was the home of smoking; and whoever has the honour of having smoked the first pipe in England, it is fairly certain that the habit was brought into common use by Sir Walter Raleigh. The practice spread rapidly among all classes of society, but chiefly were the young gallants addicted to it. And it was thought to be an essential of the man-about-town to be learned in the art of smoking and its accessories. The rich young gallant carried his apparatus about with him—tobacco-box, tobacco-tongs, ladle, priming iron, and pipes. Smoking or, as it was called, "drinking" tobacco was distinctly a fashionable accomplishment. There were indeed even "schools" on the analogy of fencing and dancing schools, where the fashionable art of smoking was taught. Ben Jonson's "Bobadil" is an amusing example of the bragging "tobacconist" or tobacco smoker; valuable illustrations of the practice will be found in Dekker's *Gul's Horne-booke;* and the practice of gallants to show off their skill with the pipe upon the stage at plays is illustrated in *The Knight of the Burning Pestle* and in *Cynthia's Revels.*

Tobacco was at once the regular demand at taverns and ordinaries but was also sold by shops of all kinds. Barnaby Rich, in *The Honestie of this Age* (1614) says that tobacco was sold in every inn, alehouse, and tavern just as beer and wine; he also says that it was "confidently reported" that in London upwards of 7000 shops lived by that trade alone. The opposition to the prevalent habit was headed by King James, and his *Counterblaste to Tobacco* makes amusing reading for those who are interested in the curiosities of literature. (The best accounts of Smoking are G. L. Apperson, *The Social History of Smoking*, and Count Corti, *History of Smoking*.)

SPITTING: compare Hentzner, a German traveller who visited England in 1598: "They have pipes on purpose made of clay, into the further end of which they put the herb, so dry that it may be rubbed into powder; and putting fire to it, they draw the smoak into their mouths, *which they puff out again through their nostrils, like funnels, along with it plenty of phlegm and defluxions from the head.*"

IT IS THE PLACE ONLY ... ENGLAND ITSELF: *i.e.* it is the only place ... The Spanish policy of James I., and the projected marriage of Prince Charles to a daughter of Philip III., were very unpopular in the country. But tobacco smokers looked upon Spain as the source of their supply, as the tobacco-growing countries were still almost entirely Spanish colonies in the New World.

HUMOURS: A play upon the two meanings of the word, (1) *moods*, *cf.* p. 120; (2) what Hentzner euphemistically calls " defluxions."

HE IS THE PIECING ...: tobacco-selling was chiefly taken over by the apothecaries or druggists, whose shops often became meeting places or " ordinaries " of smokers. But we also hear of mercers, grocers, chandlers, and others, who sold tobacco. " The druggist-tobacconists were well stocked with abundance of pipes—those known as Winchester pipes were highly popular—with maple blocks for cutting or shredding tobacco upon, juniper wood charcoal fires, and silver tongs with which the hot charcoal could be lifted to light the customer's pipe. The maple block was in constant use in those days, when the many present forms of prepared tobacco and varied mixtures were unknown. In Middleton and Dekker's *Roaring Girl* (1611), the ' mincing and shredding of tobacco ' is mentioned; and in the same play, by the way, we are told that ' a pipe of rich smoak ' was sold for sixpence." —(Apperson, *op. cit.*, p. 40.)

44. AN AFFECTED MAN.

Page 64.

TAKEN IN IT: *i.e.* his exaggeration is recognised for affectation.

CIRCUMSTANCE: formality; detail.

POINT-BLANK: exact. He overstudies his part in minute details and so becomes absurd by exaggeration.

OPINION: reputation.

PUNCTILIO: petty formality of behaviour.

45. A POT-POET.
Page 65.

FEIGN A GOD: Earle refers to the trite poetical common-place, whereby the poet asserts that he is inspired by the " divine Muse." The pot-poet is inspired by the very real god drink.

CENTOS: patchworks, or medleys constructed of borrow-ings from other authors.

ALMANAC'S: Overbury says in the Character of an *Almanac-maker:* " The verses of his book have a worse pace than Rochester hackney." The almanacs of the day pretended to prediction by astrology and were interspersed with bad verses.

ARGUMENT: subject.

MELPOMENE: the Muse of Tragedy.

POOR GREEKS' COLLECTION: After the disastrous expedi-tion of Nicias to Sicily (413 B.C.) some of the Athenian prisoners obtained mitigation of their lot, or even freedom, by their ability to recite choruses from Euripides.

NAVY: the navy, which under Elizabeth's reign had been remarkably well equipped, was allowed under James I. scandalously to deteriorate, although some improvement followed the searching Commission of 1618. This statement must therefore be sarcastic.

MEN OF TYBURN: *cf.* p. 120.

MONSTER OUT OF GERMANY: the indecent curiosity of the populace for the spectacle of monstrosities was as keen in Earle's day as it is to-day. It is satirised in *The Knight of the Burning Pestle*, III. ii. 139-44; *Tempest*, II. ii.; and Jonson's *Alchemist*, V. i.

PAINTED CLOTH: painted cloths had begun to take the place of tapestries as wall hangings in Shakespeare's time. When Mistress Quickly is threatened with the necessity of pawning the tapestry of her dining chamber Falstaff consoles her with the words: " and for thy walls, a pretty slight drollery, or the story of the Prodigal, or the German hunting in water-work, is worth a thousand of these bed-hangings and these fly-bitten tapestries."—(*2 Henry IV.*, II. i. 156.) These cloths were often inscribed with popular rhymes.

46. A PLAUSIBLE MAN.
Page 66.

MUTUALITIES: "reciprocal exchanges," that is, "intimacies."

47. A BOWL-ALLEY.
Page 67.

Despite statutes in 1511 and 1541 forbidding it, bowling continued a favourite pastime and was the occasion of gambling. In his *Schoole of Abuse* (1579) Gosson writes: "Common Bowling Allyes are privy Mothes, that eate uppe the credite of many idle Citizens, whose gaynes at home are not able to weighe down theyr losses abroad, whose Shoppes are so farre from maintaining their play, that their Wives and Children cry out for bread, and go to bedde supperlesse ofte in the yeere." The frequency with which its technical terms ("rub," "bias," "cast," etc.) are used metaphorically witnesses to its great popularity.

SCHOOLS: *i.e.* University disputations.

THE BETTERS: Shakespeare refers to gambling at bowls in *Cymbeline*, II. i. 1-8.

BEADSMEN: those who pray for the soul of another; commonly used also of almsmen.

IT IS . . . PHILOSOPHY: in this sentence Earle alludes to the four temperaments, (*a*) the melancholic, (*b*) the sanguine, (*c*) the choleric, and (*d*) the phlegmatic.

EMBLEM OF THE WORLD: Shakespeare frequently uses the game of bowls to represent the vicissitudes of fortune and the world. Cf. *Richard II.*, III. iv. 1-5; *Coriolanus*, V., II. 19-21.

WRONG-BIASED: "Bias" in bowls is used (1) of the structure and weighting of the bowl, which causes it to run in a particular curve; (2) of the twist given the bowl at casting in order to assist or counteract its natural curve; (3) of the curved course of the bowl. Cf. Shakespeare, *King John*, II. i. 574-80; *Taming of the Shrew*, IV. v. 24-5.

MISTRESS: in bowls the "mistress," or as it is now called the "jack," is the small bowl at which the others are aimed.

FORTUNE: in apposition to Mistress. Fortune is the mistress (jack) of the world.

SPITED: regarded with spite or annoyance.

TOUCHER: a technical term for the ball which is closest to the jack.

48. THE WORLD'S WISE MAN.
Page 68.

Compare Bunyan's Mr. Worldly Wiseman in *Pilgrim's Progress.*

DETERMINED IN: bounded by.

ENGINES: this word was used as we use " instruments " or " agents."

THIS THING OF FRIEND: " what it is to have a friend." Compare " this fire of wit " in No. 6 (*see* note), and " this folly of plain dealing," below.

STRIKE OFF . . . PLACE: " to obtain the honour or position of another man after causing him to lose it "; " strike off " means remove from the list.

RUBS: this metaphor comes originally from bowls, where a *rub* is any unevenness or obstruction which impedes or deflects the course of the ball. Compare *Hamlet*, III. i. 65, " Aye, there's the rub."

SFORZA: this is the name of a famous Italian family, who became dukes of Milan. West understands Earle to allude here to Ludovico il Moro (1451–1508), famous as the patron of Leonardo da Vinci. But he was surpassed in the reputation for cruelty both by his predecessor Galeazzo Maria (1444–76), who was assassinated by three Milanese noblemen enflamed by the classical example of Brutus and Cassius, and by Caterina Sforza, the illegitimate daughter of Galeazzo Maria. It is likely that Earle had no one prince in particular in mind. The very name of Sforza, like that of Borgia, was synonymous with ruthlessness and cruelty.

BORGIA: Cesare Borgia, son of Pope Alexander VI., was the greatest of the type of adventurers to which Renaissance Italy gave birth. With the Papacy behind him he led a brilliant, meteoric career, dimmed by his father's death. He was unscrupulous, ferocious, and treacherous; but his personality as a great criminal, as well as in other respects, has been exaggerated.

RICHARD THE THIRD: (1452–85), was long regarded in popular imagination as a monster of cruelty, ranking alongside the Sforzas and Borgias. While he cannot be absolved from the crime from which this reputation derived—the murder of his two nephews in the Tower— he had good qualities, both as a man and a ruler, combining culture with cruelty, capable of high ends though unscrupulous of means.

49. A SURGEON.
Page 69.

Contemporary references to surgeons are usually unflattering. In *Pierce Pennilesse* Nasshe censures the Surgeon and Apothecary together. Yet the Company of Barbers and Surgeons (formally united in 1540), was enlightened and conscientious. The barbers were excluded from all surgery except bleeding and dentistry. Careful regulations were enforced for the education and training of apprentices. And in 1572 attendance at demonstrations of anatomy were made compulsory on Fellows. "Anatomies" were performed about four times a year on the bodies of executed felons granted by the charter of 1540.

SLASHING AGE OF SWORD AND BUCKLER: "In Elizabeth's reign young gallants . . . gave up the old-fashioned sword and buckler in favour of the newer, more stylish, and deadlier rapier."—Sir Walter Raleigh (*Shakespeare's England*, Vol. I., p. 13). In *Romeo and Juliet* Benvolio carries the old-fashioned arms, and Tybalt the rapier.

LAW AGAINST DUELS: private duelling, which had reached ridiculous proportions in Elizabeth's reign, was severely discountenanced by James I. His *Proclamation against private Challenges and Combats* appeared in 1613. Henceforth the killing of an opponent in a duel was treated as murder.

MATTER: a pun, (*a*) todo, (*b*) pus.

CALAIS SANDS: In James I.'s time it was a common practice for duels to be fought abroad (and Calais was a favourite spot) in order to escape the consequences of the law. "In 1614 Bacon, the Attorney-General, delivered (before the Star Chamber) a *Charge touching Duels* . . . At the close of his speech Bacon asks that, upon his application, a writ *ne exeat regno* may be issued to stop any person from going beyond the sea for the purpose of fighting a duel."—(West).

50. A PROPHANE MAN.
Page 70.

LAW GIVES HIM LEAVE: the "blasphemy laws" which make the denial of God's being or providence punishable by fine and imprisonment, or other corporal punishment, are still unrepealed on the Statute Book.

51. A CONTEMPLATIVE MAN.
Page 71.

SCAFFOLD: from Chaucer's time until the end of the sixteenth century "scaffold" was the technical term for the platform or stage upon which plays were acted. But with the erection of permanent and more elaborate theatres it was also used, as here, of the raised gallery in which the more wealthy spectators were accommodated.

YAWNING: gaping. The word is suggestive of ignorant wonder.

52. A SHE PRECISE HYPOCRITE.
Page 72.

The meaning of the title is "Hypocritical Puritan Woman." For this use of "she" compare "she apothecary" in No. 5; and for "precise" *cf.* p. 108.

NONCONFORMIST: this word originated in the early seventeenth century (and so was quite new when Earle wrote) of "one who, while adhering to the doctrine of the Church of England, refused to conform to its discipline and practice."—(*N.E.D.*). Earle uses the word in a general sense without implication of doctrinal assent. But it is important to realise that it did not imply membership of an organised religious body which was separated from the Church of England.

STOMACHER: the front of the doublet. In Elizabeth's reign the stomacher frequently reached below the hips and was elaborately decorated. The Puritan's passion for austere costume has been already noticed (see p. 109).

RUFFLE: a small ruff (*cf.* p. 110).

GENEVA PRINT: "Strict devotees were, I believe, noted for the smallness and precision of their ruffs, which were termed *in print* from the exactness of the folds. So in

Mynshul's *Essays*, 1618: ' I undertake a warre when I adventured to speak in *print* (not *in print as Puritans' ruffes are set*).' The term *Geneva print* probably arose from the minuteness of the type used at Geneva. *Cf.* the *Merry Devil of Edmonton*, a comedy, 1608: ' I see by thy eyes thou hast bin reading little Geneva print.' "—(Bliss.) Compare also Massinger, *Duke of Milan*, I. 1: " Unless he read it in *Geneva* print, lay him by the heels." " Geneva " was a general term for whatever was distinctive of Calvinism or Puritanical. Thus Laud says: " They do not only sing the Psalms after the Geneva Tune but expound the text too in the Geneva sense." *Geneva bands* were bands resembling those worn by the Swiss Calvinist clergy; *Geneva gown* was the sort of gown worn by the Calvinist clergy when preaching; and so on. Thus " Geneva " here has a very direct reference to religious convictions. Compare Davenant, *News from Plymouth*, IV. (1673) 23/1: " your little ruff'd Geneva-Man "; and T. Adams (1633), *Exp.* 2 Peter, ii. 5: " You shall ... find her (*i.e.* Pride) as soon in a little Geneva-set, as in a great Spanish ruff."—(*N.E.D.*)

RAG OF ROME: " rag " was commonly used as a term of belittlement. *Cf.* Shakespeare, *Merry Wives*, IV. ii. 194: " You Witch, you Ragge, you Baggage."—(*N.E.D.*).

WHORE OF BABYLON: commonly applied to Rome as the centre of the Roman Catholic Religion. *Cf.* Revelation, xvii. 5; 1 Peter, v. 13.

VIRGINITY ... POPERY: allusion to celibacy of the nuns.

MARRIES ... RING: the Puritan opposition to ceremonial has already been mentioned (p. 109). They objected to the use of the ring at marriage on the ground that it was a symbol of the Roman conception of marriage as a sacrament. The use of the word " tribe " subtly implies that the Puritan custom is on a level with the marital habits of savages, or possibly of the gypsies.

FOR THE SCRIPTURE: for biblical quotations. The Nonconformist predilection for biblical quotation is not extinct. It originated from the Reformation insistence on the right of individual interpretation against traditional authority.

TWO HOURS: for lasting two hours. The length of Puritan sermons was notorious.

LECTURERS: a class of preachers usually chosen by the parish and supported by voluntary contribution. They were in general Puritans who were prevented by conscientious scruples from taking on the full duties of a parish clergyman. They preached often in the afternoons of the week and were exceedingly popular.

EXERCISE: service. Weekday services or sermons were on Wednesday, Friday, and Saturday.

GOSSIPINGS: merry-makings.

SABBATH-DAYS' JOURNEYS: there is an ironic reference to the meaning of this phrase in Scripture, viz. the furthest distance allowed by Rabbinical prescription to travel on a Sabbath; this was 2000 ells or about 1,225 yards.

FIVE MILES: alludes to the Five Mile Act.

SILENCED MINISTER: the persecution of the Puritans was revived by Archbishop Bancroft in 1604. According to Neal (*History of the Puritans*, I. i. 41-2), above 300 Puritan ministers were " silenced," or forbidden to preach, at this time.

VIRGIN MARY'S SALVATION: the Puritans were bitterly opposed to the adoration of the Virgin, as symptomatic of Popery.

FAITH . . . GOOD WORKS: alludes to St. Paul's contrast of Faith and Works, which came again to the fore at the Reformation.

SAMPLERS: exercises in embroidery, which often contained mottos or texts.

REBECCA . . . HANNAH: a skit upon the puritan fashion of using scriptural names.

VIRGINALS: a keyboard instrument, the strings of which were plucked by quills. Its tone was slight but clear. It is the ancestor of the harpsichord and modern piano.

ORGANS: in his Character of *A Puritan* Overbury says: " Shew him a ring, he runs back like a bear; a pair of organs blow him out o' th' parish."

BELLS: the strength of the Puritan aversion to bells is illustrated by John Bunyan's history, who, though passionately addicted to bell-ringing, abandoned the practice at his conversion. In *Grace Abounding*, 33, he says: " Now you must know, that before this I had taken much delight in ringing, but my conscience beginning to be tender, I thought such practice was but vain, and therefore forced myself to leave it."

THE PRACTISE OF PIETY: this is one of the two " pious books " which Bunyan's wife brought with her, and of which he says: " these books, though they did not reach my heart, to awaken it about my sad and sinful state, yet they did beget within me some desires to reform my vicious life, and fall in very eagerly with the religion of the times." It was written by Lewis Bayly (afterwards Bishop of Bangor), in 1612, and became very popular.

BROWNIST: follower of Robert Browne (1550-1633). The principles of Browne were among the most advanced of his day, and the position taken by his followers (afterwards known as Separatists) was in principle that of Congregationalism.

EXPOUNDS . . . MINISTERS: *i.e.* interprets " priests of Baal " in the Bible to refer to Reading Ministers. The great prophets of the Northern Kingdom were in continual opposition to the foreign " Baal "-religions. At the Hampton Court Conference (1604), the Puritans pressed for a " preaching ministry." Bancroft, on the other hand, dreading the effects of an increase of preaching, urged the need for a " praying ministry " and " moved that the Number of Homilies might be increased, and that the Clergy might be obliged to read them instead of Sermons, in which many vented their Spleen against their Superiors." —(Neale.)

SCOTUS: John Duns Scotus (A.D. 1265-1308) was named *Doctor Subtilis.* He was a scholastic renowned for the subtlety of his logic and the niceness of his distinctions. His name later became a by-word for quibbling.

MAYPOLE: in his *Declaration to His Subjects concerning lawful Sports to bee used* (1633) James I. especially sanctions May-games. But they were the object of the most rabid attacks of the Puritan writers, who saw in them only an occasion for license and immorality. Mayday festivities were a much more important and popular custom than they are now. In a well-known passage Stow describes Mayday in London thus: " the citizens of London . . . had their several Mayings, and did fetch in Maypoles, with divers warlike shows, with good archers, morris-dancers, and other devices for pastime, all the day long; and towards evening they had stage-plays and bonfires in the streets." The Puritan opposition is caricatured in Beaumont and Fletcher's *Women Pleased.*

PHINEAS' ACT: Numbers, xxv. 7, 8.

53. A SCEPTIC IN RELIGION.
Page 74.

PROTESTANTISM . . . ABROAD: *i.e.* men are born Protestants in England and Papists abroad. If the accident of birth thus decides a man's religion, he argues, apologetics are predecided and have no truth-value.

STARS: it was the generally accepted belief in the Middle Ages that a man's destiny was predecided by the stars which were in the ascendant when he was born. Astrology so penetrated the common and general attitude of belief that it has left innumerable metaphors in the language.

ZEAL OF AMSTERDAM: consequent upon the activities of Bancroft in 1604 many English Puritans, and especially Brownists, went abroad to the centres of Reformed religion in the Low Countries, there to found churches under the direction of their pastors.

PROPEND: incline.

FATHER'S: the early Christian writers who are accepted as authoritative.

SOCINUS: Fausto Paolo Sozzini (1559-1604), worked to give a rational simplification of the fundamental doctrines of Christianity, focusing his attack on the current ecclesiastical " superstitions " in the evangelical doctrine of Atonement. Socinianism was a very persistent bugbear of the Reformed theologies of the seventeenth century.

VORSTIUS: Conrad Vorst (1569-1622), a German theologian who succeeded Arminius as professor at Leyden. His family had been Catholic but became Protestant. However, his *Tractatus Theologicus de Deo* was strenuously attacked by the Calvinists and ordered by James I. to be burnt at Oxford, London and Cambridge.

54. AN ATTORNEY.
Page 76.

BLUE COAT: blue was the regular colour for underservants and flunkies, cf. *Taming of the Shrew*, IV. i. 93-4; *1 Henry VI.*, I. iii. 46-7.

LAWYER: barrister.

SMATCH OF A SCHOLAR: smattering of scholarship.

HARDLY: with difficulty; badly; with a pun upon the sense " cruelly."

AND LEST . . . OUT: that is, he omits the terminations of Latin words lest his ignorance of the language should be revealed by grammatical howlers. Compare Butler's Character of a Lawyer: " He has but one termination for all Latin words, and that's a dash."

SOLICITOUS: " anxious." There may be intended a pun upon " solicitor."

MOOTED: to " moot " is to debate an imaginary case of law as was done by the students of the Inns of Court as part of their training.

GIRDLE: he would carry his inkhorn and pens in his girdle.

TERM: pun: (*a*) legal term, (*b*) span.

DOOMSDAY: (*a*) Doomsday book, (*b*) Last Judgment.

SECURE: (*a*) certain, (*b*) care free.

55. A COWARD.
Page 77.

OPINION OF: reputation for.

EXCEPTIOUS: captious; peevish.

OCCASION: pretext.

BEWRAY: used in the double sense, (1) befoul, (2) betray.

56. A PARTIAL MAN.
Page 78.

RESTRAINS: restricts.

THE BEST SCHOLAR THERE: this repetition is unlike Earle; read with a strong emphasis on the second " there."

ARGUMENT . . . ANTECEDENT: conclusion . . . premise.

AFFECTIONATE: favourer; well-affected person.

HIS FACTION: what party he belongs to.

SEJANUS: ambitious and unscrupulous minister of Tiberius; executed 31 A.D.

TIBERIUS: Roman Emperor, A.D. 14-37. The picture of him as merely cruel and debauched owes its existence to the bias of Tacitus and the exultant pornography of Suetonius. In truth he was a capable ruler with definite faults, which were exaggerated in his later years.

RESPECT: " partiality." (The sense of the word in which it is said that God is no " respecter of persons.")

57. A TRUMPETER.
Page 79.

FOR HE EATS . . .: the trumpeter earns his bread by his trumpet.

PROLOGUE'S PROLOGUE: on the Elizabethan stage a trumpet was blown thrice as a signal that the play was about to commence; immediately after the third blast the " Prologue " entered, garbed in a black velvet gown and wearing a garland of bays.

COUNTERFEIT BANKRUPT: " Politicke Bankruptisme," or Fraudulent Bankruptcy, is the subject of the first section of Dekker's *Seven deadly Sins of London* (1606). Dekker describes how the scheming merchant, by punctuality at first in meeting his engagements and strict attention to business, wins a good reputation in the City, and obtains large credits. Then he bolts, or goes into hiding. " Parles are then summoned; composition offered: a truce is sometimes taken for three or four yeeres; or (which is the more common) a dishonourable peace (seeing no other remedy) is on both sides concluded, he being only gayner by such civill warres, whilst the Citizen that is the lender is the loser." Having made terms, the " counterfeit Bankrupt " comes back in triumph to the City and unblushingly sells the goods of which he has acquired possession. Thus his nominal ruin is really his gain. —(West's note.)

58. A VULGAR-SPIRITED MAN.
Page 80.

PUBLICLY AFFECTED: public favourites.

SPINOLA: *cf.* p. 123.

THE BEARS: Bear-baiting was a very popular amusement among all members of society. It was encouraged by both Elizabeth and James I. The main centre was the Bear Garden or Paris Garden, as it was called, on Bankside. Lupton has an amusing Character of Paris Garden, in *Town and Country Carbonadoed*.

59. A PLODDING STUDENT.
Page 82.

QUITTING: repaying.

AND A BODY: *i.e.* he has no intellectual talent—the one necessity for his aim.

DISPOSITION: arrangement.

LYCOSTHENES: Conradt Wolffhart (1518-61), a German philologist. His book here referred to is the commentary on *De Viris Illustribus*, at that period attributed to the younger Pliny but now thought to have been written by Aurelius Victor (fourth century A.D.).—(West.)

60. A SORDID RICH MAN.
Page 83.

DEAR YEAR: 1574. A year in the winter of which provisions were unprecedentedly dear. Holinshed ends a catalogue of abnormal prices with the smugly complacent reflection that " all this dearth notwithstanding, (thanks be to God,) there was no want of anie thing to them that wanted not money."

GREAT FROST: the frost of December 1564 was long remembered as " the great frost." An extremely vivid description of it will be found in Virginia Woolf's *Orlando* (pp. 33 ff.).

REDEEM . . . REPUTATION: sacrifice his reputation to save a penny.

61. PAUL'S WALK.
Page 84.

Paul's Walk, or Duke Humphrey's Walk, was the main aisle of St. Paul's Cathedral. " This was long the common news-room of London, the resort of the wits and gallants about town. Here lawyers stood at their pillars, like merchants on change, and received their clients. Here masterless men set up their bills for service. Here the rood loft, tombs, and font were used as counters for the payment of money, and here assignations were made. Here also ale and beer, baskets of bread, fish, flesh, and fruit were sold, and mules and horses were led, until the scandal became so great that in 1554 the Mayor and

Common Council prohibited such 'irreverent' practices. Dugdale says that Inigo Jones's portico to the west front was built 'as an ambulatory for such as usually walking in the body of the church, disturbed the solemn service in the choir.' Shakespeare and Ben Jonson have drawn the living picture of the frequenters of the place in Bardolph, bought by Falstaff 'in Paul's' (*2 Henry IV.*, I. ii. 57), and in Bobadil, 'a Paul's man' (*Every Man in his Humour*)."— (H. B. Wheatley, in *Shakespeare's England*, Vol. II., p. 166). Bliss quotes Osborne *Traditional Memoires on the Reigns of Elizabeth and James* (1658): "It was the fashion of those times (James I.) and did so continue till these (the interregnum,) for the principal gentry, lords, courtiers, and men of all professions, not merely mechanicks, to meet in *St. Paul's* church by eleven, and walk in the middle isle till twelve, and after dinner from three to six; during which time some discoursed of business, others of news."

ISLE: a pun upon "aisle," which was often spelt "isle."

EXCHANGE: allusion to the Royal Exchange.

LECTURES: *cf.* p. 164.

CHEAPEN: bargain for.

TEMPLE . . . SANCTUARY: *cf.* St. Mark's Gospel, xi. 17.

CAPTAINS OUT OF SERVICE: John Awdeley in *Fraternity of Vagabonds* (1565) describes the methods of "A Courtesy Man," who obtains money on the pretence of being a soldier from the wars. The possibility of this form of deceit shows that the soldier out of service and of work must have been a fairly common figure.

THRIFTIER MEN . . . CHEAP: it was a common joke against the penurious gallant that, unable to afford the price of a dinner in an ordinary, he would spend the dinner hour walking in Paul's Walk. This was popularly termed "to dine with Duke Humphrey."

62. A MERE GREAT MAN.
Page 85.

IMAGES: effigies of his ancestors, in Westminster Abbey.

FELLOW OF WESTMINSTER: the guide.

PARCELS OF THE CHRONICLE: portions of chronicles or histories, referring to his ancestors.

BARE HEAD: *i.e.* while they remove their caps to him in seeming reverence.

63. A COOK.
Page 86.

DRIPPINGS: dripping is the cook's perquisite.—(West.)

ROAST: the original has "roste," a pun upon "roost" and "roast."

HIS CUNNING . . . CASTLES: the seventeenth century taste for pseudo-gothic was even carried into their cookery. I have an amusing seventeenth century cookery book (of which, unfortunately, the title-page is missing), where, under "Elegant Ornaments for a Grand Entertainment," are given recipes for "A Floating Island," "Chinese Temple or Obelisk," "Desert Island," "Solomon's Temple," etc.

DARIUS' PALACE: *cf.* Dryden's *Alexander's Feast*.

MURDERER OF INNOCENTS: *cf.* St. Matthew's Gospel, ii, 16.

SAINT LAWRENCE'S GRIDIRON: St. Lawrence is a Christian martyr (festival on Aug. 10); the basilica over his tomb at Rome is still visited by pilgrims. The story of his martyrdom, related by St. Ambrose (*De Officiis*, i. 41, ii. 28), has it that he was burnt alive on a gridiron. The date is usually placed at 258 A.D. in the persecution of Valerian; but the fact of the martyrdom has been questioned.

FOUR O'CLOCK: in time to prepare dinner for six.

REGIMENT: kingship (of the kitchen).

64. A BOLD FORWARD MAN.
Page 88.

MAKE OTHER: make others think highly of him.

SNUFF: wick or burnt out candle.

ST. MARY'S: *cf.* p. 107.

REGENCY: "Every M.A. under one year's standing was expected to examine in the schools until the year 1785: the M.A.'s first year from creation was his year *necessariae regentiae;* many of the friars and monks were chased out of the university in 1537, as well as other D.D. who swore to keep a longer term of regency, and it was found necessary to add to the *necessary* regency, first *one*, and then *two* years extra, which were not absolutely binding."—(Wordsworth, *op. cit.* p. 211.)

PAUL'S CROSS: "Paul's cross stood in the church-yard of that cathedral, on the north side, towards the east end. It was used for the preaching of sermons to the populace." —(Bliss.)

ALIFE: an obsolete word (from *lief*, dear) found only in the phrase "love alife"—love dearly.

BENJAMIN'S MESS: Genesis, xliii. 34.

SCULLER: Thames boatman.

SCARLET: *i.e.* Doctor's degree.

65. A BAKER.
Page 89.

VERIFIES: proves the truth of.

PENALTY . . . DOLE: "A royal charter, granted in 1307, empowered the London Bakers' Company to weigh all bread sold within twelve miles of the city, and if they found it not of due assize to distribute it to the poor of the parish in which it was seized."—(West.)

PILLORY: the pillory was a method of punishment used particularly against defaulting tradesmen and notorious shrews.

HEARS WELL: (1) this may refer to the custom of nailing the ears to the pillory when the offence was severe. (2) It may be used simply in the sense " have a good reputation."

66. A PRETENDER TO LEARNING.
Page 90.

KNOW SO MUCH: (*a*) know as much as he; (*b*) know that he knows nothing.

CONCEITS . . . OPINION: desires only the reputation.

SENECAS: there are two Senecas: (1) Annaeus Seneca, father of the following and grandfather of Lucan. He was a famous rhetorician and composed a collection of declamations, which is partially extant. (2) Lucius Annaeus Seneca (*circa* 5 B.C.—65 A.D.), the most famous Roman philosophical writer after Cicero. Many of his letters, philosophical treatises, epigrams, and tragedies have survived.

TACITUS: (*circa* 54 A.D.–118 A.D.). The most famous historian of the Empire from Tiberius to Domitian. He writes in a pithy epigrammatic style.

PARCELS: scraps.

AUSTIN: common syncopated form of "Augustine," Bishop of Hippo, and Father of the Church (354-430).

SCALIGER: Joseph Justus Scaliger (1540-1609), was the greatest scholar of his day. He was the first to apply sound rules of criticism and emendation, and changed textual criticism from a series of haphazard guesses to a scientific study with rational principles. He also revolutionised accepted ideas of ancient chronology. Scaliger was perhaps the greatest master of erudition who has ever lived, though of critical scholarship he perhaps had less than Casaubon.

CASAUBON: Isaac Casaubon (1559-1614), a self-taught Greek scholar, was recognised to be after Scaliger the most learned authority of his day in classics. He is still remembered as one of the outstanding philologists and commentators. His correspondence with Scaliger is a unique document of the happy relations between two of the greatest scholars of all time, and his *Ephemerides* or diary is the most valuable record we have of the daily life of a man of letters in the sixteenth century. In 1610 Casaubon came to England at the invitation of Bancroft, and that King James I. might flatter his own tastes for scholarship by conversations with so famous a scholar. He was buried in Westminster Abbey.

JESUITS: aspired to be the source of all scholarship and criticism. They attacked both Scaliger and Casaubon.

UNDER ARMINIUS: below the standing of Arminius. (*Cf.* p. 124.)

67. A POOR MAN.
Page 91.

Compare the following, from Wye Saltonstall's Character of *The World:* "Poverty is accounted as spreadingly contagious as the Plague; he that is affected with it is shunned of all men, and his former friends look upon him as men look upon dials with a skew countenance, so finding him in the afternoon of his fortunes pass by him. Acquaintance is here chosen with the bravest not with the wisest; and a good suit makes a man good company."

SHARKING: sponging. *Cf.* No. 19.

VIZARD: mask; deception; or the modern use of "façade."

SPECULATION: insight; view.

HOLIDAY: special; out of the ordinary.

68. A HERALD.

Page 93.

The function of the heralds consisted in the granting (and invention) of coats of arms, the recording and tracing of pedigrees, and the supervision of funerals. The College of Heralds was first incorporated under a charter of Richard III. in 1483, and received a second charter in 1555. At the head of the College was the Earl Marshall, and below him three "kings," six "heralds" and four "pursuivants." By the sixteenth century a coat of arms had come to be the accepted voucher of gentility, and the avidity for heraldic honours and the facility with which they were granted to those who could pay is frequently ridiculed in contemporary drama.

BLOOD: used in the sense of "nobility."

FIELDS: a technical term in heraldry.

OR AND ARGENT: heraldic names (from the French) of gold and silver.

RAMPANT: a play upon the heraldic meaning (standing upon the left hind leg with both the forelegs elevated, the right above the left, and the head in profile); exorbitant; extravagant.

BRAWNS: boars.

HE WAS SOMETIMES . . .: "Heraldry was a flower of medieval war; and Tudor fashions had no place for it in the line of battle . . . Heraldry still coloured the mimic warfare of tournaments."—(Oswald Barron, in *Shakespeare's England*, Vol. II., p. 74.)

WALES: the intricate family ramifications of the Welsh are proverbial. Overbury makes the same point in *A Braggadochio Welshman*.

69. THE COMMON SINGING-MEN IN CATHEDRAL CHURCHES.

Page 94.

SYNTAXIS: "order." A pun upon "syntax."

RESIDENCER: residentiary; incumbent.

ORGANS: pun (*a*) church organs, (*b*) organs of the body.

70. A SHOPKEEPER.
Page 95.

TITLE-PAGE OR INDEX: *i.e.* the exposition of the contents.

WHAT THEY LACK: the usual phrase of a shopkeeper. *Cf.* Dekker, *The Honest Whore, First Part*, I. v.: " Gentlemen, what do you lack ? "

MAKES A GAIN ... GODLINESS: *cf.* 1 Timothy, iv. 8.

71. A BLUNT MAN.
Page 95.

MASTERS: the ordinary form of address, which has deteriorated into " Mister."

SQUEAZY: sparing.

72. A HANDSOME HOSTESS.
Page 97.

MEN OF IRON: warriors.

ROARERS: swashbucklers.

CONFUSION: pouring out, consumption.

POTTLE: tankard.

LITTLE JUGS: A " jug " was a measure, usually about a pint; " little jugs " means " short measure."

INFIDEL: disbeliever.

73. A CRITIC.
Page 98.

CRITIC: philologist (in the European sense); classical scholar.   Compare Overbury's Character of *A Pedant*.

DESUNT MULTA: inserted in a classical text to indicate a large gap in the MS.

HE RUNS ... SYNTAXIS: scientific books were ordinarily written in Latin. He reads them merely to inspect the orthography.

SOPHISTICATE: adulterated; degenerated from a primitive purity. Thus if Attic Greek is " genuine " (pure), Hellenistic Greek is " sophisticate."

ENTOMBED BY VARRO: Marcus Terentius Varro (116-27) was the most learned scholar, antiquarian, and philologist of the Romans, and one of the most voluminous writers of antiquity. Of his great work on the Latin language in 35 books (*De Lingua Latina*), books V-X survive in a mutilated condition. His other grammatical writings are lost.

OMNEIS: the accusative plural of third declension nouns is written " es " or " is." The critic supposes that the original form was " eis " and so writes " omneis."

QUICQUID: a pedantic affectation for the more usual " quidquid."

GERUND: West writes: " The Critic's gerund may be described as ' incomformable ' because it resists attraction, —remains a gerund and does not become a gerundive. Or Earle may have had in view passages in which the gerund of transitive verbs with *est* governs an object,—an idiom affected by Varro: e.g. *agendum est hanc rem*. Or, again, he may have been thinking of such constructions as *poenarum solvendi tempus* (*Lucretius* V. 1225), *principium generandi animalium* (Varro, *De Re Rustia*, II. i.). Both these usages are fairly described as ' incomformable.' "

74. A SERGEANT, OR CATCH-POLE.

Page 98.

RUN ... THROUGH: *i.e.* with a sword.

HANDSEL: first-fruits; or first experience.

KING'S NAME: because he arrests in the King's name.

75. AN ORDINARY HONEST MAN.

Page 99.

BEGINS TO: pledges; toasts.

LIKELY: either " like himself," or " able to look after himself."

HONEST FELLOWS: *i.e.* in the sense Earle has defined— but not *truthful*.

76. AN UNIVERSITY DUN.
Page 100.

TOO WEAK . . . MODESTLY: " too small a claim to take to court, so he arrests you in a modest way." There is a play upon " arrest " in the legal sense and in the general sense (now archaic) " accost."

USE UPON YOUR NAME: *i.e.* runs up a bill in your name.

77. A STAID MAN.
Page 101.

DISTINCT: defined; well ordered.

SAY AFTER: repeat something on the authority of.

IN A BRAVERY: from bravado.

OLD ROUND BREECHES: worn especially by the City merchant class during Elizabeth's reign. There was, however, at the time when Earle wrote a tendency for the fashion to change towards greater frivolity and for the citizen to ape the fashions of the court gallant.

CAREFUL WITHOUT MISERY: frugal without miserliness.

WELL POISED . . . HUMOURS: a good balance of all (four) temperaments.

78. A SUSPICIOUS OR JEALOUS MAN.
Page 103.

WATCHES HIMSELF A MISCHIEF: is on the look-out for an insult or injury.

LEER: looking askance; sly,